FENELON'S TREATISE ON THE EDUCATION OF DAUGHTERS

First published 1805
This edition published by Lector House in 2024

ISBN: 978-93-6138-942-9

Lector House LLP
Registered Office: H. No. 96, Block C, Tomar Colony,
Burari, Delhi – 110084, India
info@lectorhouse.com
www.lectorhouse.com

FENELON'S TREATISE ON THE EDUCATION OF DAUGHTERS

FRANÇOIS DE SALIGNAC DE LA MOTHE-FÉNELON,
THOMAS FROGNALL DIBDIN

2024

LECTOR HOUSE LLP

Delightful task! to rear the tender thought,
To teach the young idea how to shoot.

FENELON'S TREATISE ON THE EDUCATION OF DAUGHTERS:

TRANSLATED FROM THE FRENCH, AND ADAPTED TO ENGLISH READERS,

WITH AN ORIGINAL CHAPTER, "ON RELIGIOUS STUDIES."

BY

THE REV. T. F. DIBDIN, B.A. F.A.S.

Author of
"An Introduction to the Knowledge of the best Editions of the Greek and Latin Classics," &c.

"Chaste and modest writings never alter the honour of any gentlewoman. For as the remembrance of infamous persons is much detested and hated by the *Muses*—so is the glory and renown of the virtuous installed by them in eternal memory for ever."

PASTORALS OF JULIETTA. *Fol. Edit.* 1610.
Pt. 3, *p.* 88.

So in this pilgrimage I would behold
You, as you are—Virtue's Temple!

DONNE'S POEMS. *Edit.* 1650. *p.* 156.
[*To the Countess of Bedford.*]

TO

HER GRACE GEORGIANA

DUCHESS OF BEDFORD,

WHOSE AMIABLE DISPOSITION,

ACCOMPLISHED MANNERS,

AND

ELEVATED RANK,

RENDER HER

THE ESTEEM AND ADMIRATION

OF

THE GREAT AND THE VIRTUOUS,

This small Tribute

OF GRATITUDE AND RESPECT

IS DEDICATED

BY HER OBLIGED

AND OBEDIENT HUMBLE SERVANT,

H. RUFF.

Preface.

The Translation of the following Work was undertaken at the request of Mr. RUFF, the Publisher, who wished me to paraphrase what I thought might more particularly interest and edify the English reader.

It is dedicated, by the Publisher, to her Grace the DUCHESS OF BEDFORD—and he is anxious that it may be found worthy of her patronage.

The original French work was first published in 1688; and the earliest English translation appeared in 1707. This translation, which was by Dr. Hickes, I have never seen. In the year 1797, another [anonymous] English translation was printed at Hull, in a duodecimo volume. In this performance there is so close an adherence to the idiom of the French language, that almost every page abounds with gallicisms. It is not, however, entirely destitute of merit; but it appears, on the whole, to have been hastily executed for the purpose of ensuring a cheap and extensive sale.

The present translation is offered to the public, with a full conviction of its inadequacy to give a just idea of the beauty and force of the original. The author of "*Telemaque*" and "*De l'Education des Filles*" appears, on a comparison of these two performances, very unlike the same writer. In the former, his periods are flowing and luxuriant; in the latter, they are sententious and logical; and nearly as difficult to clothe in an English-dress as those of the philosophical Tacitus.

It will be seen, therefore, that a literal translation has not been attempted; and a still greater deviation will be observable, from a wish to distinguish it from the translation of 1797. Whether this has always been done for the better, the reader will determine for himself.

The *Original Chapter* "ON RELIGIOUS STUDIES" has been submitted to those, whose opinions, matured by experience, I have been anxious to obtain; and it has received the sanction of their approbation.

If the Work fail of success, it will not be from the want of spirit in the Publisher; for it is accompanied with considerable beauty of type and paper, and elegance of ornament.

The *design* is every way worthy of the ingenious artist by whom it was executed, and who has long been known to the world from the taste and fidelity of his pencil. The engraving, by Mr. Freeman, will convince the public that he requires only to be known, to be more generally encouraged.

T. F. D.

TERRACE, KENSINGTON,
June 2, 1805.

Contents

FENELON ON
FEMALE EDUCATION.

Chapter I.

On the Importance of the Education of Daughters.

The Education of Girls is, in general, exceedingly neglected:[1] custom, and maternal caprice, often appear to have the entire regulation of it. It absolutely seems as if we supposed the sex to be in need of little or no instruction. On the other hand, the Education of *Boys* is considered as a very important concern, affecting the welfare of the public; and although it be frequently attended with errors and mistakes, great abilities are nevertheless thought necessary for the accomplishment of it. The brightest talents have been engaged to form plans and modes of instruction:—What numbers of masters and colleges do we behold? What expences incurred in the printing of books, in researches after science, in modes of teaching languages, in the establishment of professors? All these grand preparations may probably have more shew than substance, but they sufficiently denote the high idea we entertain of the education of Boys. In regard to Girls, some exclaim, "why make them learned? curiosity renders them vain and conceited: it is sufficient if they be one day able to govern their families, and implicitly obey their husbands!" Examples are then adduced of many women whom science has rendered ridiculous; and on such contemptible authority we think ourselves justified in blindly abandoning our daughters to the conduct of ignorant and indiscreet mothers.

---

[1] It must be remembered that the above sentiment was expressed in the year 1688, when the want of a good system of female education was universally felt and regretted. At the present day, we witness a noble reverse of things; and whatever theories may have, been proposed abroad, we can never cease to admire the labours, and applaud the sagacity, of *our* countrywomen in behalf of their sex.

It is true, that we should be on our guard not to make them ridiculously learned. Women, in general, possess a weaker but more inquisitive mind than men; hence it follows that their pursuits should be of a quiet and sober turn. They are not formed to govern the state, to make war, or to enter into the church; so that they may well dispense with any profound knowledge relating to politics, military tactics, philosophy, and theology. The greater part of the mechanical arts are also improper for them: they are made for moderate exercise; their bodies as well as minds are less strong and energetic than those of men; but to compensate for their defects, nature has bestowed on them a spirit of industry, united with a propriety of behaviour, and an economy which renders them at once the ornament and comfort of home.[2]

But admitting that women are by nature weaker than men, what is the consequence? What, but that the weaker they are, the more they stand in need of support. Have they not duties to perform, which are the very foundation of human existence? Consider, it is women who ruin or uphold families; who regulate the *minutiæ* of domestic affairs; and who consequently decide upon some of the dearest and tenderest points which affect the happiness of Man. They have undoubtedly the strongest influence on the manners, good or bad, of society. A sensible woman, who is industrious and religious, is the very soul of a large establishment, and provides both for its temporal and eternal welfare. Notwithstanding the authority of men in public affairs, it is evident, that they cannot effect any lasting good, without the intervention and support of women.

The *world* is not a phantom, it is *the aggregate of all its families*; and who can civilize and govern these with a nicer discrimination than women? besides their natural assiduity and authority at home, they are peculiarly calculated for it, by a carefulness, attention to particulars, industry, and a soft and persuasive manner. Can men promise themselves any felicity in

[2] This idea is beautifully expressed in the following lines of THOMSON:—

"To give society its highest taste,
Well-ordered home man's best delight to make;
And by submissive wisdom, modest skill,
With every gentle care-eluding art
To raise the virtues, animate the bliss,
And sweeten all the toils of human life:
This be the female dignity and praise!"

Autumn, ver. 602-608.

this life, if marriage, the very essence of domestic society, be productive of bitterness and disappointment? and as to children, who are to constitute the future generation, to what misery will *they* be exposed, if their mothers ruin them from the cradle?

Such then, are the occupations of the female sex, which cannot be deemed of less importance to society than those of the male. It appears that they have a house and establishment to regulate, a husband to make happy, and children to rear. Virtue is as necessary for men as for women; and without entering upon the comparative good or ill which society experiences from the latter sex, it must be remembered that they are *one half of the human race*, REDEEMED BY THE BLOOD OF JESUS CHRIST, AND DESTINED TO LIFE ETERNAL.

Lastly, let us not forget that if women do great good to the community when well educated, they are capable of infinite mischief when viciously instructed. It is certain that a bad education works less ill in a male, than in a female breast; for the vices of men often proceed from the bad education which their mothers have given them, and from passions which have been instilled into them at a riper age, from casual intercourse with women.

What intrigues does history present to us—what subversion of laws and manners—what bloody wars—what innovations in religion—what revolutions in states—all arising from the irregularities of women? Ought not these considerations to impress us with the importance of female education? Let us, therefore, discuss the various means of accomplishing so desirable an object.

Chapter II.

Errors in the Ordinary Mode of Education.

Ignorance is one of the causes of the *ennui* and discontent of young persons, and of the absence of all rational amusement. When a child has arrived at a certain age without having applied to solid pursuits, she can have neither taste nor relish for them. Every thing which is serious assumes to her mind a sorrowful appearance; and that which requires a continued attention, wearies and disgusts her. The natural inclination to pleasure, which is strong in youth—the example of young people of the same age, plunged in dissipation—every thing, in short, serves to excite a dread of an orderly and industrious life. In this early age, she wants both experience and authority to take a decided part in the management of household affairs; she is even ignorant of the important consequences resulting from it, unless her mother has previously instructed her in some of its departments. If she be born to affluence, she is not necessitated to undergo manual toil: she may probably work an hour or two a day, because she hears it said, without knowing why, that "it is proper for women to work"—but this pithy proverb will only produce the semblance, without the substance, of real useful application.

In such a situation what is she to do? The society of a mother, who narrowly watches, scolds, and thinks she is performing her duty in not overlooking the least fault—who is never satisfied, but always trying the temper, and appears herself immersed in domestic cares; all this disgusts and torments her. She is, moreover, surrounded with flattering servants, who, seeking to insinuate themselves, by base and dangerous compliances, gratify all her fancies, and direct her conversation to every topic but that of goodness and virtue. To her, piety appears an irksome task—a foe to every rational amusement. What, then, are her occupations? None that are useful. Hence arises a habit of indolence, which at length becomes incurable.

Meantime what is to fill this vacuity? Nothing but the most frivolous and contemptible pursuits. In such a state of lassitude, a young woman abandons herself to pure idleness; and idleness, which may be termed a languor of the soul, is an inexhaustible source of weariness and discontent. She sleeps one-third more than is necessary to preserve her health: this protracted slumber serves only to enervate and render her more delicate; more exposed to the turbulency of passion; whereas moderate sleep, accompanied with regular exercise, produces that cheerfulness, vigour, and elasticity of spirits, which form, perhaps, the true criterion of bodily and mental perfection.

This weariness and idleness, united with ignorance, beget a pernicious eagerness for public diversions; hence arises a spirit of curiosity, as indiscreet as it is insatiable.

Those who are instructed and busied in serious employments, have, in general, but a moderate curiosity. What they know gives them an indifference for many things of which they are ignorant; and convinces them of the inutility and absurdity of those things, with which narrow minds, that know nothing, and have nothing to exercise themselves upon, are extremely desirous of becoming acquainted.

On the contrary, young women, without instruction and application, have always a roving imagination. In want of substantial employment, their curiosity hurries them on to vain and dangerous pursuits. Those who have somewhat more vivacity, pique themselves on a superior knowledge, and read, with avidity, every book which flatters their vanity: they become enamoured of novels, plays, and "Tales of Wonder," in which love and licentiousness predominate: they fill their minds with visionary notions, by accustoming themselves to the splendid sentiments of heroes of romance, and hence are rendered unfit for the common intercourse of society; for all these fine airy sentiments, these generous passions, these adventures, which the authors of romance have invented for mere amusement, have no connexion with the real motives which agitate mankind, and direct the affairs of the world; nor with those disappointments which usually accompany us in almost every thing we undertake.

A poor girl, full of the tender and the marvellous, which have delighted her in her reading, is astonished not to find in the world real personages, resembling the heroes she has read of—fain would she live like those imaginary princesses, whom fiction has described as always charming, always adored, and always beyond the reach of want. What disgust must she feel on descending from such a state of heroism, to the lowest offices of housewifery!

Some there are who push their curiosity still further, and without the least qualifications, presume to decide upon theological points.—But those who have not sufficient grasp of intellect for these curiosities, have other pursuits, better proportioned to their talents: they are extremely desirous of knowing what is said, and going on in the world—a song—news—an intrigue—to receive letters, and to read those that other people receive; these things delight prodigiously; they wish every thing to be told them, and to tell every thing in turn: they are vain, and vanity is a sure incentive to talk. They become giddy, and volatility prevents those reflections from rising which would shew them the value of silence.

Chapter III.

Of the First Foundations of Education.

To remedy the evils just complained of, it is of material consequence to commence a system of education from *Infancy*: this tender period, which is too often intrusted to imprudent and irregular women, is, in truth, the most susceptible of the strongest impressions, and consequently has a great influence on the future regulation of life.

As soon as children can lisp, they may be prepared for instruction: this may be thought paradoxical—but only consider what a child does before it can talk. It is learning a language which it will, by and by, speak with more accuracy, than the learned can speak the dead languages, although studied at a mature period of life. But what is the learning a language? It does not consist solely in treasuring in the memory a great number of words—but in comprehending, says St. Austin, the meaning of each particular word: the child, amidst its cries and amusements, knows for what object each word is designed: this is obtained sometimes by observing the natural motions of bodies which touch, or shew, the objects of which one is speaking—sometimes by being struck with the frequent repetition of the same word to signify the same thing. It cannot be denied but that the brain of children is admirably calculated, from its temperament, to receive impressions from all these images; but what strength of mental attention is requisite to distinguish them, and to unite each to its proper object?

Consider too, how children, even at such a tender age, attach themselves to those who flatter, and avoid those who restrain, them: how well they know to obtain their object by a tear, or silent submission: how much artifice and jealousy they already possess! "I have seen," exclaims St. Austin, "a jealous child: it could not speak; but its face was pale, and the eyes were irritated against an infant that suckled with it."

From this it may be inferred, that infants know more at such an early period than is usually imagined: thus, by soft words and appropriate gestures, you may incline them towards honest and virtuous connexions, rather than introduce them to those which it would be dangerous for them to caress.—Thus, again, you may, by appropriate looks and tone of voice, represent to them, with horror, those whom they have seen exasperated with anger, or any other furious passion; and, on the other hand, by a correspondent serenity of manner, depicture to them those who are amiable and wise.

I do not wish to lay too great a stress on these subordinate matters: but, in reality, these different dispositions form a commencement of character which must not be neglected; and this mode of foreseeing, as it were, the future dispositions of children, has imperceptible consequences which facilitate their education.

If we still doubt of the power of these early prepossessions on future maturity, we need only call to mind how lively and affecting, at an advanced age, is the remembrance of those things which have delighted us in childhood. If, instead of terrifying the minds of young people with absurd notions of ghosts and spirits, which serve only to weaken and disturb the still delicate texture of the brain: if, instead of abandoning them to the caprice of a nurse for what they are to like or dislike, we endeavoured always to impress on their minds an agreeable idea of good, and a frightful one of evil—this foresight might hereafter be the foundation of every practical virtue. On the contrary, we frighten them with the idea of a clergyman clothed in black—we talk of death merely to excite terror—and recount tales of the dead revisiting the earth, at midnight, under hideous shapes! All this has a tendency to weaken and agitate the mind, and to excite a prejudice against the soundest doctrines.

One of the most useful and important things during infancy is, to be particularly careful of the child's health; endeavouring to sweeten the blood by a proper choice of food, and a simple regimen of life: regulating its meals, so that it eat pretty nearly at the same hours, and as it feels the inclination; that the stomach be not overloaded before digestion takes place, and that no high-seasoned dishes be introduced, which must necessarily give a disrelish for more healthful food. Lastly, too many dishes should not be allowed at the same time; for such a variety of food begets an appetite even after the real call of hunger is satisfied.

Another very important consideration is, not to oppress the faculties by too much instruction; to avoid every thing which may kindle the passions; to deprive a child, gently and by degrees, of that for which it has expressed too vehement a desire to obtain; so that, eventually, it may be insensible of disappointment.

If a child's disposition be tolerably good, it may, by the foregoing method, be rendered docile, patient, steady, cheerful, and tranquil; whereas, if its tender years be neglected, it becomes restless and turbulent during the remainder of its life; the blood boils, bad habits are formed, and the body and mind, both equally susceptible, become prone to evil. Hence arises a sort of second original sin, which, in advanced age, is the source of a thousand disorders.

As soon as children arrive at a more mature period, or their reason becomes unfolded, we must be careful that all our words have a tendency to make them love truth, and detest artifice and hypocrisy. We ought never to be guilty of any deception or falsehood to appease them, or to persuade them to comply with our wishes: if we are, we instruct them in cunning and artifice; and this they never forget. Reason and good sense must be our instruments of regulation.

But let us examine with a little more attention the exact dispositions of children, and what more particularly regards their treatment. The substance of their brain is soft, but it becomes harder every day: it has neither experience nor judgment to discriminate one object from another, and every thing is, therefore, new to them. From this softness and pliability of the brain, impressions are easily made; and the surprize which accompanies novelty, is the cause of their continual admiration, and extreme curiosity. It is true that this ductility of the brain, attended with considerable heat, produces an easy and constant motion; hence arises that bustle and volatility of youth, which is as incapable of fixing the attention on one object, as it is of confining the body to one spot.

Again, children are incapable of thinking and acting for themselves; they remark every thing, but speak little; unless they have been accustomed to talk much—an evil, against which we must be constantly on our guard.

The pleasure which we derive and express from the sight of *pretty children*, spoils them; for they are, in consequence, accustomed to utter every thing which comes uppermost, and to talk on subjects of which they have no distinct ideas; hence is formed an habit of precipitately passing judgment, and of discussing points they are incapable of comprehending; an unfortunate circumstance! and which, probably, adheres to them through life.

This admiration of *pretty children* has another pernicious consequence; they are sensible that you look at them, watch all their actions, and listen to their prattle, with pleasure—hence they flatter themselves that all the world must follow your example.

During this period, when applause is perpetually bestowed, and contradiction seldom obtruded, children indulge chimerical hopes, which, alas! are the source of endless disappointments throughout life. I have seen children who always fancied you were talking about them, whenever any thing was privately said—and this, forsooth, because it has *sometimes* actually been the case: they have also imagined themselves to be most extraordinary and incomparable beings. Take care, therefore, that in your attentions to children, they are unconscious of any particular solicitude on your part: shew them that it is from pure regard, and the helplessness of their condition to relieve their own wants, that you interest yourself in their behalf—and not from admiration of their talents. Be content to form their minds, by degrees, according to each emergency that may arise: and if it were in your power to advance their knowledge much beyond their years, even without straining their intellect, by no means put it in practice; recollect that the danger of *vanity* and *arrogance* is always greater than the fruit of those premature educations which make so much noise in the world.

We must be satisfied to follow and assist nature. Children know little, and should not be stimulated to talk: but the consequence of this ignorance is, they are continually asking questions. We should, therefore, answer them precisely, and add sometimes little comparisons, which may throw light on the information we give them. If they judge of some things without sufficient knowledge, they should be checked by a new question, which might make them sensible of their error without rudely confounding them; at the same time take care to impress on their minds, not by vague praises, but by some effectual mark of esteem, that they afford much more satisfaction when they *doubt*, and *ask for information*, on points they do not know, than when they happen to decide rightly. This is the sure method to implant in them a true sense of modesty and politeness; and to excite a contempt for those idle controversies in which ignorant young folks are too apt to indulge.

As soon as we begin to watch the dawn of reason spreading, we should seize it as a favourable opportunity to guard them against presumption: "You see," we should exclaim, "that you are much more reasonable and tractable than you were last year—and in the *following* year you will observe things yet more clearly than you do at present—if, during the last year, you were eager to have passed judgment on things which you now know, and were then ignorant of, you would assuredly have judged wrong. You would therefore have been to blame in offering opinions on subjects above the reach of your intellect. There are, at this moment, many things which remain for you to know; and you will one day be convinced how imperfect are your *present* conceptions. Nevertheless, adhere to the counsel of those who judge of things as you yourself would judge, were you gifted with their years and experience."

As the curiosity of children is a faculty which precedes instruction, we should be careful to make them profit by it. For example, in the country when they see a mill, they wish to know what it is—here, then, you may shew them how that food is prepared which nourishes man. A little further they perceive reapers—and you must explain to them their occupation; how they sow the grain, and how it multiplies in the earth. In the town they see a number of shops, where various trades are exercised, and various merchandize is sold. Never consider their questions as importunate; they are overtures which nature makes to facilitate instruction—shew them, therefore, that you take pleasure in these questions—for, by such means, you teach them insensibly how every thing is made, which conduces to the comfort of man, and extension of commerce. By degrees, and without any particular study, they become acquainted with every article that is useful, and with the price affixed to each, which is, indeed, the true foundation of economy. This kind of knowledge, which no one should despise, because no one is willing to be cheated from the want of it, is particularly necessary for women.

Chapter IV.

The Danger of Imitation.

The ignorance of children, (in whose brain no correct impressions are made,) renders them extremely susceptible, and inclined to imitate every thing they see. It is, therefore, of consequence to set before them none but the very best models of imitation; and to make them acquainted with those, by whose examples they would be profited in following. But as it happens, in spite of all our precautions, that they occasionally witness many irregularities, we must not fail to warn them betimes against the impertinence of certain foolish and dissipated people, whose reputation is scarcely worth preserving: we must shew them how truly miserable and deserving of contempt, are those who abandon themselves to passion, without cultivating their reason. One may also give them, a correct taste, free from affectation, and make them sensible of the true value of modesty and decorum; we must not even abstain from guarding them against probable errors, although by this means we may open their eyes to certain defects in those whom they are taught to respect. We have neither right nor reason to hope that they will remain ignorant on such points, and therefore the best method to pursue, in order to keep them to their duty, is, to persuade them to bear with the faults of others; not to pass too severe a sentence on them, as they often appear greater than they really are—that they are even compensated for by many good qualifications—and that as there is no perfection in this world, they should admire that which approaches the nearest towards it. Lastly, although this advice should not be offered but in extreme cases, we should, nevertheless, engraft on them *true principles*, and preserve them from imitating all the evil that is set before them.

We must also be on our guard to prevent their imitation of *ridiculous people*; whose low and buffoon-like manners have something in them extremely revolting to noble and generous sentiments; we should be apprehensive lest children afterwards assume these very manners; as the warmth of their imagination, and pliability of body, added to the pleasure they seem to take in such diversion, gives them a peculiar aptitude to represent every ridiculous object they behold.

This proneness to imitation, which is natural to children, is the source of infinite mischief when they are delivered up to improper people who are hardly able to restrain themselves before them. But providence has ordained this imitative power, that children may be also capable of applying themselves to what is good and virtuous. Often, without speaking to them, we have only to *shew* them in others what we would have them do themselves.

Chapter V.

Indirect Instructions: We should not be too urgent with Children.

I think we should often make use of *indirect* instructions, which are not so tedious and uninteresting as lessons and remonstrances, in order to excite their attention to certain examples which are placed before them.

A person may sometimes ask another, in their presence, "Why do you do so"—and the other may answer—"I do it for such a reason." For example—"Why did you confess your fault?" "Because I should have been guilty of a much greater one by disavowing it with a lye"—and because nothing is more praiseworthy than to say frankly, "I am wrong." Then the first person should commend the one who has thus accused herself—but care must be taken that all this be done without art or affectation, for children have much more penetration than we are aware of—and as soon as they discover any finesse in their teachers, they lose that simplicity and confidence which is natural to their character.

We have before observed that the brain of children, from being at the same time moist and warm, produces continual motion. This softness or pliancy of the brain causes impressions to be easily made, and images of every sensible object to be vividly and strongly imprinted; hence we should be anxious to engrave, as it were, on their minds such characters as are easily formed. But great care must be shewn in the selection of such objects as we wish to impress: for in so small and precious a cabinet, none but the most exquisite furniture should be admitted. Let it be remembered, that at such a tender age, no knowledge should be engrafted but such as we wish to remain there for life. The first impressions that are made, when the brain is so soft and susceptible, are in general the most durable; and in proportion as age hardens the brain, do such impressions become indelible. Hence it is, that in old age we remember distinctly the images of youth, however remote; whereas as age advances we have a fainter recollection of such things as we progressively behold, because the impression has been made on the brain when it is gradually hardening, and filled with other images.

Although we understand how to reason in this manner, we have some difficulty in acceding to it: and yet we absolutely do make use of this very mode of reasoning. For instance, do we not say every day, "My habits are fixed, I am too old to change them, I have been brought up in this way."—Moreover are we not conscious of a singular pleasure in recalling to mind the images of youth? are not the strongest propensities formed at that age? Does not, therefore, all this prove that the first impressions and first habits are the strongest? If infancy be the fittest period for engraving such images on the brain, it must be allowed that it is the least so for the cultivation of reason. That ductility of the brain which causes impressions to be easily formed, being united with extreme heat, produces an agitation which sets all regular application at defiance.

The brain of children may be compared to a lighted wax taper, situated in a place which is exposed to the wind—its flame is perpetually flickering. A child asks you a question, and before you can answer, its eyes are directed towards the cieling: it counts all the figures that are carved there, or all the bits of glass which compose the window: if you wish to bring it back to the first subject of discussion, you vex it as much as if you confined it in prison. Thus great care is required in managing the organs before they assume a determined inclination: answer every question promptly, and leave the child to put others as it pleases. Gratify only the curiosity which it evinces, and lay up in the memory a mass of sound materials. The time will come, when these impressions will be regularly arranged, and the brain having more consistency, the child will reason on the consequences. Nevertheless, be attentive to correct when the reasoning is fallacious; and to convince it, without embarrassment, as an opportunity offers, in what a wrong consequence consists.

Let a child amuse itself freely, and mingle instruction with amusement: let wisdom be introduced at proper intervals, and under an agreeable form; and take care not to fatigue it by a precision which is both formal and injudicious.

If a child entertains sad and dismal notions of virtue, if liberty and irregularity present themselves in a seducing manner, every thing is lost, and your labour is in vain. Never suffer it to be flattered by little contemptible associates, or people without character or worth: we naturally love the manners and sentiments of those whom we regard; and the pleasure which is sometimes taken in the company of disreputable people, begets, by degrees, a love of those pernicious habits which renders *them* so truly contemptible.

In order to conciliate children to people of real estimable character, make them reflect on their excellence and utility, their sincerity, their modesty, their disinterestedness, their fidelity, their discretion, but above all their *piety*, which is the foundation of the rest.

If a child has any thing about it revolting or offensive, you must observe to it that "piety does not produce such defects: when it is perfect, it destroys, or at least softens them." But, after all, we must not persist in making children admire certain pious characters whose exterior deportment is disgusting.

Although you are particularly anxious to regulate your own conduct with the utmost circumspection and nicety, do not imagine that children will fancy you faultless: oftentimes your slightest imperfections will be noticed by them.

St. Austin informs us that he had remarked, from his infancy, the vanity of his tutors. The best and most politic thing you can do, is, to know your own faults as completely as a child will know them, and to request some real friend to warn you of them. The generality of instructors pardon nothing in a pupil, but every thing in themselves: this excites an inquisitive and watchful spirit of malignity in such pupils—so that whenever they detect any fault in their tutor, they are delighted, and eventually despise him.

Shun this error: do not be afraid to mention the faults which are visible in your conduct, and which may have escaped you before the child. If you find her capable of reasoning thereupon, observe that you set her an example of correcting her faults, by the detection of your own—by this means, your imperfections will be instrumental in edifying the child, and encouraging her to correct herself. You will also thereby avoid the contempt and disgust which your own faults may cause her to entertain against your person.

Meanwhile, try every method to make those things agreeable which you exact from a child. Have you any thing crabbed or difficult to propose? convince her that this pain will be succeeded by pleasure: always shew the utility which results from your instructions; and make her sensible of the consequences as affecting mankind, and the different orders of society. Without this, all study will appear as a dry, barren, and thorny path. "Of what use," will children sometimes say to themselves, "is it to learn those things which do not relate to ordinary conversation, and which have no immediate connection with what we are *obliged* to do?"

We should therefore give them a reason for every thing we teach—"It is, we should observe, to enable you one day to do well in the world—it is to form your judgment, and to make you reason well on all the affairs of life." We should always represent to them some useful and solid *end*, which may support them in their application: and never pretend to keep them in subjection by a crabbed and absolute authority.

In proportion as their reason advances, we should discuss with them on the necessity of education; not that we should implicitly follow their thoughts, but profit by them when they discover their real state of mind: so that we may try their discernment, and make them relish those things we are anxious for them to learn.

Never assume, without urgent necessity, an austere and imperious manner, which only causes children to tremble, and savours strongly of affectation and pedantry in those who govern: children are, for the greater part, timid and diffident. By such means you shut out all access to the heart, and deprive them of a confidence, without which no benefit can be derived from instruction. Make yourself beloved: let them be free with you, so that they fear nothing in discovering their faults. In order to attain this, be indulgent to those who do not disguise themselves before you. Appear neither astonished nor irritated at their bad propensities: on the contrary, bear with their foibles. This inconvenience may, however, sometimes arise, that they will be less intimidated; but, taking all things together, confidence and sincerity is of far greater utility than a rigorous discipline.

Besides, authority will lose its proper effect, if confidence and persuasion are not equally strong. Always commence with an open and candid manner; be cheerful and familiar without vulgarity, which enables you to see children conduct themselves in a perfectly natural state, and to know their inmost character. If even you should succeed in all your plans by the force of authority alone, you will not gain the proper end: you will disgust them in their search after goodness, of which you ought solely to endeavour to inspire them with admiration.

If the wisest man has recommended parents to hold the rod continually over the heads of their children, if he has said that a father who "spareth his child" will repent it hereafter—it does not follow that he has censured a mild and lenient mode of education. He only condemns those weak and inconsiderate parents who flatter the passions of their children, and who only strive to divert them in their infancy, so that they are guilty of all sorts of excess. The proper conclusion seems to be that parents ought to preserve authority sufficient for correction; for there are some dispositions which require to be subdued by fear alone; but let it be remembered that this should never be enforced unless every other expedient has been previously applied.

A child who merely follows the capricious impulse of imagination, and who confounds every thing which presents itself to her mind, detests application and virtue, because she has taken a prejudice against the person who speaks to her concerning them.

Hence arises that dismal and frightful idea of religion, which she preserves all her life: and which, alas! is often the only wretched remnant of a severe system of education. We must frequently tolerate many things which are deserving of immediate punishment, and wait for the opportunity when the feelings of a child dispose it to profit by correction.

Never rebuke a child in the first moments of passion, whether on your side or hers. If on yours, she will perceive that, you conduct yourself according to caprice and resentment, and not according to reason and affection: you will, in consequence, irretrievably lose your authority. If you correct in the first gust of her passion, her mind is not sufficiently collected to confess her fault, to conquer her feelings, and to acknowledge the importance of your advice: such a mode may even hazard your pupil's respect for you. Always let the child see you are mistress of your own feelings; and nothing can effect this so much as *patience*. Watch every moment, each day, when correction may be well-timed. Never tell her of a fault, without, at the same time, suggesting some mode of redressing it, which will induce her to put it in practice; for nothing is more to be avoided than that chagrin and discouragement which are the consequence of mere formal correction. If a child is discovered to be a little rational, I think you should win it insensibly to *wish* to have its faults disclosed, as this would be the way of making it sensible of them, without causing affliction: never, however, recount too many faults at a time.

We should consider that children have a tender intellect, that their age makes them susceptible chiefly of pleasure, and that we often expect from them a correctness and seriousness of deportment, which their instructors are sometimes incapable of evincing. A very dangerous impression of *ennui* and sadness is produced on their mind, by perpetually talking to them of words and things which they do not understand: no liberty, no amusement! always lesson, silence, constraint, correction, and threats!

Our ancient forefathers knew better. It was by the charm of verses and music that the Hebrews, Egyptians, and Greeks, introduced the principal sciences, the maxims of virtue, and the politeness of manners. Without reading, people scarcely believe these things, so distant are they from present custom! nevertheless, little as history is known, there is not a doubt but that this was the common practice for many centuries. However, let us so far correct our own age, as to unite the agreeable and the useful together, as much as lay in our power.

But although we can hardly hope to lay aside *awe* with the generality of children, whose dispositions are headstrong and untractable, we should, nevertheless, not have recourse to it without having patiently tried every other experiment. We should even make them distinctly understand the extent of our demands, allowing a certain medium with which we should be satisfied: for good-humour and confidence should be their natural disposition—otherwise we damp their spirit, and daunt their courage: if they are lively, we irritate; if dull, we stupify them.—Fear may be compared to violent remedies employed in extreme cases—they purge, but they alter the temperament, and reduce the organs to extremity. A mind governed by fear, is generally the weaker for it.

We should not always menace without chastising, for fear of rendering menace of no avail; but we should menace more frequently than we chastise. As to chastisement, the pain inflicted ought to be as slight as possible—but accompanied with every circumstance which can prick the child with shame and remorse. For example, shew her every thing you have done to avoid coming to this unpleasant extremity—appear to be even affected at it—speak to her, in the presence of others, of the melancholy state of those whose want of reason and good conduct have forced correction upon them; and keep back the ordinary marks of reconciliation, till you see she stands in need of consolation. This chastisement may be either public or private, as it may benefit the child—either in covering her with shame, or shewing her how she has been spared such a mortification—a *public* exposition should, however, never be resorted to but in the last extremity. It may be as well sometimes to make use of a rational person to perform the office of mediator—who might console the child, and mention such things which would be improper for yourself to do—who might cure her of false shame, and induce her to come to you for reconciliation—and to whom the child, in the emotions of her heart, would open herself more freely than she would dare to do to yourself. Above all, let it be manifest that you never exact from a child more than necessary submission: endeavour to effect it so that she may pass her own condemnation, and that you have little else to do but assuage the anguish she has herself inflicted. General rules ought to be adopted as particular occasions may justify: men, and especially children, do not always resemble themselves—that which is good to-day, may be bad to-morrow; a conduct stubbornly uniform can never be advantageous.

The fewer formal lessons that are inculcated, the better. A thousand modes of instruction may be adopted in the freedom of conversation, more useful than lessons themselves. I have known many children who have learnt to read during their play; we need only relate to them some diverting story from a book opened in their presence, and make them insensibly become acquainted with their letters; after this, they will themselves be anxious to arrive at the source which has afforded them such amusement.

There are two circumstances which spoil every thing; namely, teaching them at first to read in a foreign tongue[3]—which takes away all pleasure in reading; and making them read with a forced and ridiculous emphasis. Give them a book handsomely bound, with neat cuts, and printed with a fine type; every thing which delights the fancy, facilitates study: we should even let them have a book full of short and marvellous stories. After this, do not be uneasy about the child's learning to read—do not fatigue her by requiring too great a precision; let her pronounce naturally as she speaks: other tones are always bad, and partake of the declamation of the stage. When the tongue has acquired sufficient volubility, the chest strength, and the habit

[3] Fenelon says the *Latin* tongue: but this is not practised in England.

of reading been confirmed, she will then read without pain, and with more grace and distinctness.

The manner of teaching to write should be pretty nearly the same. When children can read a little, one may amuse them in making them sort the letters; and if there are several pupils, emulation may be kindled. Children are naturally inclined to make figures on paper; and if this propensity be encouraged, without teasing them too much, they will form letters during their play, and accustom themselves by degrees to write. One may also encourage them by the promise of a reward adapted to their taste, and which has no unpleasant consequences.

"Write me a note," you may say, "inform your brother or cousin of such and such things:" all this (varied as you like) pleases a child, provided that no sad idea of a formal lesson intrude. "A free curiosity," says St. Austin, from his own experience, "excites the mental faculties of a child, much more than the formality of rules, or a constraint imposed by fear."

Observe this grand defect in ordinary educations—all pleasure is placed on one side, and pain on the other: the latter is attached to study, the former to play. What then can be expected from a child, but that, in supporting one of these maxims, she will eagerly fly to her amusements?

Let us try to invert this order: let us make study agreeable, concealing it under the form of liberty and pleasure: the dull routine of continued application may be sometimes broken in upon by little sallies of amusement. Children require these relaxations to preserve the elasticity of their mind.

Let their imaginations roam a little. Permit occasionally some game or diversion, so that ample bounds be given to their spirits; then bring them gently back again to the principal object you have in view. Too rigid or too long continued an application to study, is productive of much injury: those who affect this regularity, act more from the convenience of stated hours of discipline, than from wishing to seize every favourable moment of instruction. At the same time, do not suffer any amusement which may agitate the passions of children: on the contrary, every thing which can unbend their faculties, produce an agreeable variety, satisfy a curiosity for useful things, and exercise their body in healthful recreations, should be recommended and practiced in their diversions. The amusements which they like best, are those that keep the body in motion; they are happy if they can but skip from place to place: a shuttle-cock or a ball is sufficient. We should not, however, be uneasy about their diversions; they invent quite enough themselves—it is sufficient if we leave them to their own inventions, watch them with a cheerful countenance, and moderate them when they become too violent. It would be prudent just to make them sensible, as much and as often as we can, of the pleasure which results from the cultivation of the *mind*; such as conversation, news, histories, and many industrious games which include instruction. All this will have its proper effect in due time: but we should not force the feelings of children on this subject; we should only make overtures to them. The period will arrive when their bodies will be inclined to move less, and their minds, more.

The care which is taken to season study with amusement, will operate favourably in abating the ardour of youth for dangerous diversions. It is subjection and *ennui* that beget an impatience for amusement. If a daughter felt less restraint in the presence of a mother, she would not be so anxious to steal away in search of indifferent society.

In choosing diversions, care must be taken to avoid all suspicious companions. Boys must not mingle with girls; even girls of an unruly and froward disposition must be rejected. Games which excite passion, and thoughtlessness, or which produce an improper attitude of the body—frequent visiting abroad, and conversations which give rise to such visits—should be uniformly avoided. When a child is not spoilt by any rude diversion, or is not stimulated by any ardent passion, it will easily find pleasure and content: health and innocence are the sure sources of both: but those who have been accustomed to violent amusements, lose all relish for moderate pleasure, and weary themselves in a restless search after happiness.

There may be a satiated taste for amusements, as well as for food: one may be so accustomed to high-seasoned dishes, that a simple and common diet will become flat and insipid. Let us, therefore, be on our guard against those violent exercises, which in the end produce *ennui* and disgust: above all, they are to be particularly dreaded in regard to *children*; who are less capable in suppressing their feelings, and who wish to be in perpetual motion. Let us manage them so as to excite a taste for simple things: that great preparations of food be not necessary for their nourishment, nor violent diversions for their amusement. A moderate fare always creates a sufficient appetite, without being obliged to pamper it with *made dishes*, which produce intemperance. "Temperance," says an ancient writer, "is the best contriver of luxury: with this temperance, which begets health of body and mind, one always enjoys a soft and tranquil emotion—there is no need of trick or public shew, or expense, to make one happy: some little diversion, or reading, or labor—a walk, or innocent conversation, which relaxes after toil—all or any of these produce a purer delight than is felt from the most exquisite music."

It is true, simple pleasures are less lively and interesting than violent ones, which elevate the soul, and affect all the sources of passion. But simple pleasures have a better tendency; they produce an equal and lasting joy, without any bitter consequence. They are always of real service, whereas violent ones may be compared to adulterated wine, which pleases at first, but which eventually injures the health. The very temperament of the soul, as well as the taste, is affected by seeking after such violent and seductive pleasures. All that you can do for children who are under your regulation is, to accustom them to such a simple life as has been just described; to fortify them in such habits as long as you can, to make them foresee the evil consequences attached to other amusements, and not to abandon them to *themselves*; as is too commonly the case, at an age when their passions begin to be shewn, and when, consequently, they stand in need of greater restraint.

It must be allowed, that of all the vexations incidental to education, none can be compared with that which is experienced in the rearing of a *stupid* child. Those who have strong lively natural capacities are, indeed, liable to terrible irregularities—passion and presumption master them entirely; but, on the other hand, they have great resources, and may be easily checked, however turbulent. Education is, in them, a concealed but vegetating germe, which sometimes bears fruit when experience comes to the aid of reason, and when the passions begin to cool. At least we know how to make them attentive, and awaken their curiosity: they have something in them which makes them take an interest in their lessons, and stimulates their sense of honour—whereas one has no sort of pleasure or gratification in the instruction of *stupid* children. All their thoughts are distracted: they are never where they ought to be: the most poignant correction has no effect on them: they hear every thing, and feel nothing. This indolence and stupidity makes a child negligent and disgusted with every thing she does. She is in such a case, that the *best mode* of education runs a risk of miscarrying, if we do not guard against the evil, from earliest infancy. Many people who have little depth of penetration, conclude, from this bad success, that nature does *every thing* in the formation of men of merit, and education *nothing*—instead of remarking that there are dispositions, like barren soils, on which cultivation produces little. It is yet more lamentable when these knotty systems of education have been thwarted or neglected, or badly regulated at the beginning.

We must not forget that there are many dispositions among children, in which we are likely to be deceived. They appear at first interesting, because there is attached to early youth a certain fascinating lustre which covers every thing: we, at first, perceive nothing but what is tender and amiable, and this prevents a closer examination of the features of the mind. Every sally of their wit surprises us, because we do not expect it at such an age: every error in judgment is permitted, and it has, moreover, the charm of ingenuity: they assume a certain vivacity of deportment, which never fails to pass for sprightliness and intellect. Hence it is, that childhood often promises much, but realises little. Such a one was celebrated for her wit at five years of age, but now, in proportion to her growth, she has fallen into obscurity and contempt! Of all the qualities which children possess, there is but one on which you can calculate with certainty, and that is, *good sense*: this "grows with their growth," provided it be well cultivated. The graces of infancy fade away—its vivacity diminishes—and that tenderness of heart even becomes blunted, in proportion as the passions and an intercourse with designing men harden young people on their entrance into the world. Strive, therefore, to discover midst the graces of childhood, whether the disposition you have to manage be deficient in curiosity, and insensible of honest emulation. If this should be the case, it is almost impossible for every one concerned in her tuition, not to be disgusted with so rugged and ungrateful an occupation. Every qualification of a child should be roused and brought into action, in order to extricate it from so fatal a lethargy. If, however, you foresee any such consequences about to follow, do not at first be anxious to urge any serious application: take care not to overcharge her memory, for it is that which stuns and stupifies the brain: do not harass her with unpleasant regulations: make her as cheerful as you can, because she labours under the opposite extreme of presumption: do not be afraid of shewing her, with discretion, the extent of her powers: be satisfied with little at a time: make her remark the smallest success: shew her how absurd it is to be afraid of not succeeding in that which she really does well: set her emulation to work. Jealousy is more violent among children than we are aware of: we often see some who are absolutely fretting and wearing away, because others are more beloved and caressed than themselves. Mothers are often cruel enough to fan this jealous flame, which, however, is of service in extreme cases of indolence and stupidity—but then you should set before the child the examples of those who are but *very little* superior—for disproportionate examples of those who are greatly superior, serve only to discourage and dismay.

Let her, occasionally, gain some little victories over those of whom she is jealous: make her, if you can, laugh heartily with yourself at her timidity: and set before her those, equally timid with herself, who have conquered their disposition to fear: make her sensible, by indirect instructions, and the example of others, that timidity and idleness destroy all the mental energies; but be careful not to give these instructions in an austere and impetuous manner: nothing wounds the inmost feelings of a mild and timid child so much as boisterous treatment: on the contrary, let the application which becomes indispensible, be seasoned and relieved by such little circumstances of amusement and recreation as are suited to her disposition. Perhaps it will be sometimes necessary to check her by reproaches; but this should not be done by yourself: employ some inferior person, or another child, without appearing yourself to be acquainted with it.

St. Austin relates, that his mother was once reproached by a servant for drinking pure wine; an ill habit which she had contracted from her infancy, and of which she was cured by the servant's reproach, though all the vehemence and severity of her governess was unable to effect it. In short one should endeavour to excite *a taste* in the minds of such sort of children, in like manner as one tries to excite it in the palate of those who are sick. *They* are permitted to have any thing which may cure their loathing; they are indulged in many whims at the expence of certain prescribed rules, provided it be not carried to a dangerous excess. It is much more arduous to create a taste in those that are void of one, than to regulate the taste of those who have not a correct one.

There is another kind of sensibility extremely difficult and important to impress them with, and that is, *friendship*. As soon as a child is susceptible of it, there can be no doubt but that you should turn her heart towards those who may be useful to her. Friendship will give her every accomplishment that you desire; you have then a certain tie on her, if you know how to regulate it: excess, or a bad choice, are the only things you have to dread. There are, however, some children who are born cunning, reserved, and callous, and who bring every thing home, as it were, to their own bosoms: they deceive their parents, whom fondness has made credulous: they *appear* to love them: they regulate their inclinations to conform to them: they *seem* more docile than other children of the same age, who indulge, without restraint, in all their humours and follies: their suppleness, or rather hypocrisy, which conceals a savage temper, assumes a softness of character; and their real disposition does not discover itself till it is too late to reform it.

If there really be any child on whom education is incapable of producing a good effect, it is one of the foregoing description; and it must be allowed that the number is greater than we imagine. Parents bring themselves with difficulty to believe that their children have a bad heart: when they shut their *own eyes* upon them, no other person will have the courage to convince them of it; and thus the evil is hourly augmenting. The principal remedy is, to place children, from their earliest infancy, in such a situation where their tempers may be discovered without disguise. Always know the very bottom of their heart, before you correct them. They are naturally simple and open; but as soon as you plague them, or give them an example of disguise, they will no longer return to their original simplicity. It is true, that a good and tender-hearted disposition comes from God alone; *we* can only endeavour to excite it by generous examples, by maxims of honour and disinterestedness, and by a contempt of those people who set too high a value on themselves. We must endeavour to make children betimes sensible of the most natural modes of conduct, and of the pleasure arising from a cordial, and reciprocal friendship. Nothing so much conduces to this end, as an intercourse with people who have nothing about them harsh, severe, low, or selfish: children might better associate with those who have other faults, than with those who possess the foregoing ones. We should praise them for every thing they do on the score of friendship, provided it be not misplaced or too violent. Parents must likewise appear to them to be animated with the sincerest friendship towards them; for children oftentimes learn of their parents to have no affection for any one object. In short I would check, before friends, all superfluous compliments, all artificial demonstrations of esteem, and all feigned caresses: for by these things you teach them a great deal of deceit towards those whom they ought to regard.

There is a very common fault among girls, the opposite to what we have been mentioning; namely, the affecting to be uncommonly struck and delighted with the most insignificant things. They cannot see two people who are both equally bad, without taking the part, in their hearts, of one against the other. They are full either of affection or aversion, without the least cause: they perceive no defect in what they esteem, and no one good quality in what they despise. You must not, at first, make a formidable opposition to all this—for contradiction will only fortify them in their vagaries: but observe, by degrees, to a young girl, that you know better than herself what good there is in that which she likes, and what evil in that which she detests. Take care also, occasionally, to make her sensible of certain defects which are sometimes found in the object of her regard, and of certain good qualities which are discernible in that of her hatred: do not be too urgent: press her not too much, and you will find that she will come to herself, and coincide with your sentiments. After which, make her reflect on her past caprices, and the most unreasonable circumstances attending them: tell her, gently, that she will by and bye see those of which she is not yet cured, when they cease to act. Recount to her similar errors of *your own* when you was of her age. Above all, shew her as clearly, and as sensibly as you can, that good and evil are inherent in every object of our love and aversion: this will repress her ardour in the indulgence of either the one or the other.

Never promise children, by way of reward, fine clothes or dainties; this has two direct evils attending it: the first will teach them to set a value on what they ought to despise; the second deprives you of an opportunity of establishing *other* rewards which would facilitate your labour. Be on your guard against threatening them to make them study, or subjecting them to any formal rule. Make as few rules as possible: and when there is an absolute necessity for one, make it pass lightly under the child's notice, without giving it such a name; and always give some reason why a thing is done at one time and in one place, rather than in another. You run a risk of disheartening children if they are not praised when they have done well. Praise may sometimes be apprehended on account of its exciting vanity; but it should nevertheless be employed to animate, not to intoxicate, children.

We find that St. Paul has often made use of it, in encouraging the weak, and in softening his reproaches. The Fathers have also made the same use of it. It is true, that to make it serviceable, it must be so tempered that it take away all exaggeration, and flattery, and that the good resulting from it be attributed to God alone, as the source. Children may be recompensed by innocent and industrious games; by walks and recreations, in which conversation may take a useful turn: by little presents which may be a kind of prize—as pictures, prints, medals, maps of geography, or gilt books.

Chapter VI.

Of the Use of History for Children.

Children are passionately fond of marvellous tales: one sees them every day transported with joy, or drowned in tears, at the recital of certain adventures. Do not fail to profit by this propensity. When you find them disposed to listen to you, relate to them some short and pretty fable: but choose some ingenious and harmless one respecting animals: repeat them just as they are composed, and shew them the moral resulting therefrom. As to *pagan fables*, a girl will be happy in her total ignorance of them, as they are extremely indelicate and replete with impious absurdities. If, however, you are not able to keep a child ignorant of them, impress her with a sense of their horror. When you have repeated one fable, wait till you are asked to begin another—thus leaving the child hungry, as it were, for more mental food. When curiosity is at last excited, recount certain choice histories, but in as few words as possible: connect them together, and postpone the sequel from one day to another, so that you keep the children in suspense, and impatient to know the termination. Be animated and familiar in your manner of repeating—make the personages speak—and children, who have a lively imagination, will fancy they hear and see them. For instance, relate the history of Joseph—make his brothers speak like brutal characters, but Jacob like a tender and afflicted father—then let Joseph himself speak—taking pleasure, as being at the head of an Egyptian establishment, in concealing himself from his brothers—in making them afraid of him; and, at last, in discovering himself to them. This natural representation, joined to the extraordinary circumstances of the history, will delight a child; provided she be not teased with too many similar recitals. You may let her express a desire for such stories, and promise them as a recompense for a prudent conduct, provided they assume not the form of study—provided the child is not *obliged* to repeat them; for these repetitions, if not voluntarily undertaken, will discompose and fret her, and take away all pleasure arising from such sort of narrations.

It must be observed that if a child has any facility in speaking, she will, of her own accord, relate to those whom she likes, such histories as have pleased her most: but do not let her make a rule of it. You may employ some one, who is on a footing of perfect intimacy with the child, to appear anxious to learn of her a particular story: the child will be delighted in repeating it. Do not appear yourself to listen very earnestly to it—let her go on as she likes, without checking her in her faults. The consequence will be, that when she is more accustomed to repeat, you may gently make her sensible of a better manner of narrating, by rendering it short, simple, and easy; and by a choice of circumstances better calculated to represent forcibly the nature of each thing. If you have many children, accustom them by degrees to *represent* the historical characters whom they read of—one may be Abraham, the other, Isaac. These representations will charm them more than any other games—will accustom them to think, and to utter serious things with pleasure—and will indelibly fix such histories on their memory.

We should strive to give them a taste for scriptural history rather than for any other; not in *telling* them that it is finer, which they will probably not believe—but in causing them to *feel* it to be so. Make them observe how important, wonderful, and curious those histories are: how full of natural representation, and a spirit of noble simplicity. Those of the creation, the fall of Adam, the deluge, the call of Abraham, the sacrifice of Isaac, the adventures of Joseph (which have been briefly discussed), and the birth and flight of Moses, are not only calculated to awaken the curiosity of children, but in discovering to them the origin of religion, fix the foundations of it in their bosoms. We must be strangely ignorant of the essential parts of religion not to observe that they are chiefly historical: it is by a tissue, as it were, of marvellous facts that we discover its establishment, its perpetuity, and all that can induce us to believe and to practice it. It is not to be supposed that by all this we wish children to be plunged into profound knowledge—on the contrary, these histories are short, various, and calculated to please the meanest capacity. The Almighty, who best knows the faculties of that being whom he has created, has clothed religion in *popular facts*, which, far from overpowering the simple, assists them in conceiving and retaining its mysteries. For example, tell a child, that in God there are three equal persons, but of one nature: by the habit of hearing and repeating these terms, she may retain them in her memory; but I doubt whether she will understand the sense of them. Relate to her that as Jesus Christ went up out of the waters of Jordan, the Almighty caused these words to be heard—"This is my beloved son in whom I am well pleased—hear him:" add, that the Holy Ghost descended on our Saviour, in the form of a dove—and thus, you make her sensible of the TRINITY, in a history which she will never forget. Here are *three persons* which she will distinguish by the difference of their actions; you have nothing more, therefore, but to inform her that all these together make but one God. This example is sufficient to shew the use of history. Although it may *seem* to make instruction more tedious, it really abridges it; and renders the dryness of catechism, where mysteries are detached from facts, unnecessary. We may observe that history was an ancient mode of instruction. The admirable method which St. Austin has pointed out for the instruction of the ignorant, was not suggested by that father alone—it was the universal method and practice of the church: it consisted in shewing, by a succession of historical facts, religion to be as ancient as the world—Jesus Christ conspicuous in the Old Testament, and pervading every part of the New: which, in truth, is the foundation of christian instruction.

All this demands a little more time and care than are devoted to the usual habits of instruction with which many people content themselves: but in adopting such a mode, religion will be truly taught; whereas, when children are not so instructed, they have only confused ideas of Jesus Christ, the Gospel, the church, of the necessity of absolute submission to its decrees, and of the foundation of those virtues with which the christian character should inspire us. The *historical* catechism, which is simple, short, and more perspicuous than the ordinary catechism, includes every thing necessary to be known thereupon—so that it need not be said that much study is necessary.[4]

Let us now add to the facts before mentioned from scripture, the passage of the Red Sea, and the sojourning of the people in the desert—where they ate bread which fell from heaven, and drank water which Moses caused to flow from the rock, by striking it with his rod. Represent the miraculous conquest of the promised land, where the waters of Jordan went backwards toward their source, and the walls of a city fell down of themselves in the

[4] I have omitted the remark which here follows—because it alludes to the catechism of the *Council of Trent*, with which we have nothing to do in this country.

sight of the besiegers. Describe, in as natural colours as possible, the combats of Saul and David: and how the latter, a youth, without arms and habited like a shepherd, became the conqueror of the fierce and gigantic Goliah. Do not forget the glory and wisdom of Solomon: how he decided between the two women who disputed about a child—but do not forget to impress on the mind, how he fell from this height of wisdom; dishonouring himself by an effeminacy, which is almost the inevitable consequence of overgrown prosperity.

Next make the prophets, as delegated from heaven, converse with kings: shew how they read the future as if in a book: how they suffered continual persecution for having spoken the truth. Speak, in succession, of the first destruction of Jerusalem—represent the temple burning, and the holy city in ruins on account of the sins of the people. Relate the Babylonian captivity, and how the Jews wept "when they thought on Sion." Before their return, represent the interesting adventures of Tobit, Judith, Esther, and Daniel. It may not be amiss to let children give their opinion on the different characters of these holy persons, to know which of them they admire the most. One will prefer Esther, the other Judith—and this may excite a little controversy between them, which will impress those histories more strongly on their minds, and form their judgments thereupon. Afterwards, bring back the Jews from captivity to Jerusalem, and make them repair their desolated city; then paint, in smiling colours, the peace and happiness which succeeded. Shortly you will have to draw a picture of the cruel Antiochus, who died in false repentance: describe, under this persecutor, the victories of the Maccabees, and the martyrdom of the seven brothers of that name.

Descend regularly to the miraculous birth of St. John: and relate, more in detail, that of our Saviour Jesus Christ: after which you must select in the four Gospels all the remarkable occurrences of his life—his preaching in the temple at twelve years of age—his baptism—his retreat and temptation in the desert—the calling of the apostles—the miracle of the loaves—the conversion of the sinful woman, who anointed the feet of our Saviour with a precious perfume—washed them with her tears, and dried them with her hair. Represent the Samaritan woman instructed; Lazarus restored to life; and Christ's triumphant entry into Jerusalem. Next describe his passion, and his resurrection from the tomb. Afterwards make them remark the familiarity with which he continued forty days with his disciples, until they saw him ascend into heaven. Next will follow the descent of the Holy Ghost; the stoning of Stephen; the conversion of St. Paul; and the calling of the centurion Cornelius: the voyages of the apostles, and particularly of St. Paul, are *yet* extremely interesting. Select the most wonderful histories of the martyrs, and give a general outline of the celestial life of the first christians: mingle with it the courage of young virgins, the astonishing austerity of those who led a solitary life, the conversion of emperors and of the empire, the blindness of the Jews, and the punishment which yet awaits them.

All these histories (managed with discretion) of the whole series of religion, from the creation to the present time, would make an agreeable impression on the lively and tender minds of children; and would fill them with such noble ideas of it as would never be forgotten. They would even see, in this narration, the hand of God always lifted up to protect the good, and to punish the wicked. They would accustom themselves to behold the Almighty, working all in all, secretly directing the movement of creatures however remote from himself. But care must be taken to select such passages in these histories as afford the most beautiful and magnificent images; for every faculty must be employed to shew religion to children adorned with every thing amiable, pleasing, and august; and not to represent it, as is too commonly the case, as something sad and disagreeable.

Besides the inestimable advantage of teaching religion in this manner to children—such a series of pleasant histories, which they learn betimes to remember, awakens their curiosity for serious things; makes them sensible of the pleasures of the mind, and excites an interest in the hearing of *other* histories which have some connection with those they already know. But again I repeat, never make a *rigid law* that they should hear and retain these things—much less let them be inculcated as *regular lessons*: for the pleasure which they take in such recitals should be *voluntary*, and without this, nothing important can be effected. Do not urge them much—you will attain the desired end, even with ordinary understandings:[5] you have nothing to do but exercise their capacities *moderately*, and let their curiosity be excited, by degrees. But you will say, how are those histories to be repeated in

[5] I may be permitted to add, that if children do not discover any propensity to these studies, we should neither neglect nor despise them; provided their dispositions and conduct be good and regular in other matters. Besides, nothing conclusive can, at first, be drawn from their inattention to these subjects; for a child at *twelve* years of age may evince as great a *regard* for them, as she did *indifference*, at *ten*. There is little consistency in the human intellect at such a volatile period: the girl of gaity and dissipation at *eighteen*, may become the devotee at *five and twenty*. T.

a lively, short, natural, and agreeable manner? Where are the teachers who can accomplish such a thing? To this I answer, that I propose it only that you should *endeavour* to choose persons of an excellent understanding to govern your children, and that they be gifted, as much as possible, with this method of teaching: every governess will undertake it in proportion to her talents. But if there be only a candour and openness of intellect, the thing will go on with good effect when children are formed to this manner, which is natural and simple.

To discourse or description, may be added the sight of *pictures*, which represent sacred subjects. Prints will be sufficient, which may be preserved for ordinary use—but when an opportunity offers of shewing a child *good paintings*, it must not be neglected: for the force of colouring, and the grandeur of composition, will strike the imagination with greater effect.

Chapter VII.

Of Inculcating Principles of Religion in the Minds of Children.

It has been before observed that the first years of childhood are not calculated for reasoning: not that children are divested of those ideas and general principles of reason which hereafter become manifest, but that they are ignorant of many facts, which hinders the application of their reason; and, moreover, leaves that agitation of the brain, which prevents them from connecting their ideas.

We should, however, without pressing them, gently direct the use of their reason towards a knowledge of God. Persuade them of Christian truths, without giving them subjects of doubt. They observe some one to be dead: they know that burial afterwards follows: say to them—"Is this dead person in the tomb?" "*Yes.*" "He is not then in paradise?" "*Pardon me, he is.*" "How can he be in the grave and in paradise at the same time?" "*It is his soul which is in paradise—his body only in the grave.*" His soul and body then are not the same thing?" "*No.*" "The soul, therefore, is not dead?" "*No—It will live for ever in heaven.*" Add: "And you, do you wish to be saved?" "*Yes.*" "But what is being saved?" "*It is the soul's going into paradise.*" "And what is death?" "*It is the mouldering of the body into dust, when the soul has left it.*"

I do not pretend to say that children may *at first* be taught to answer in this manner: though I may add that many have given me such answers when they were four years of age. Let us, however, suppose a child to be extremely reserved and uninstructed:—the worst that can happen is, the waiting only a few more years with patience.

Shew children a house, and make them comprehend that this house did not build itself. The stones or bricks, say you, were not elevated without some one's carrying them so high. It may be as well, too, to shew them the masons at work: then make them contemplate heaven and earth, and the principal things which God has made for the use of man: say to them "how much more beautiful and better made is the world than a house! Was it made of itself? No—assuredly it was made by the hands of the Almighty."

First follow the method of scripture. Strike their imaginations in as lively a manner as possible—propose to them nothing which may not be clothed with sensible images. Represent God as seated on a throne—with eyes more brilliant than the rays of the sun, and more piercing than the lightning—represent him with ears that hear every thing; with hands that support the universe; with arms always stretched out to punish the wicked; and with a tender and paternal heart to make those happy who love him. The time will come when this information may be rendered more exact. Observe every opening of the mind which a child presents to you: try her by different methods, so that you may discover how these great truths will best occupy her attention. Above all, talk of nothing new, without familiarising her to it by some obvious comparison.

For example—ask her if she would rather die than renounce Jesus Christ—she will answer—*Yes*. Then say—"how, would you suffer your head to be cut off in order to enter paradise?" *Yes.* The child will now think she has sufficient courage to do it. But you, who are willing to make her sensible that nothing can be effected without *grace*, will gain nothing, if you merely say that grace alone is sufficient to produce faithfulness—the child does not understand those words; and if you accustom her to repeat them without understanding them, you gain nothing by it. What then is to be done? Relate to her the history of St. Peter: represent him saying, in a presumptuous tone of voice—"I will follow thee even unto death, though all the rest should desert thee, yet will I never abandon thee." Then describe his fall: he denies his master, Christ, three times—even a servant makes him tremble. Declare why God permitted this weakness—then make use of the comparison of a child or sick person who cannot walk alone—and make her comprehend, that as an infant must be supported in the arms of its nurse, so we stand in need of the Almighty's assistance. Thus you will make her sensible of the mystery of grace.

But the most difficult truth for a child to comprehend is, that we have a soul more precious than our body. Children are at first accustomed to talk about the soul; and the custom is advantageous—for this language, which they do not understand, is perpetually exciting them to have a (confused) notion of the distinction of body and soul, until they are able really to conceive it. In proportion as early prejudices are pernicious when they lead to error, so are they useful when they conduct the imagination to truth, until reason is gradually directed towards it by the force of principles. But, at length, we must fix *a true persuasion*—and how are we to set about it? Is it in plunging a young girl in philosophical subtleties? Nothing is worse calculated for it. We must confine ourselves to render clear and distinct to her mind, what she hears and speaks every day.

As to her *person*, she is perhaps too well instructed in the knowledge of *that*: every thing induces her to flatter, adorn, and idolise it. An essential point is gained if you can inspire her with contempt for it, by observing something of greater value about her.

Say then to a child who is capable of a little reasoning—Is it your soul that eats? If she answers absurdly, do not be harsh with her—but tell her mildly that the soul does not eat—It is the body that eats—the body, which resembles the brutes. Have brutes intellect—are they learned? *No*, the child will answer. But they eat, you will add, although they have no intellect: you see, therefore, that it is not the soul which eats—it is the body which takes food to nourish it—it is *that* which walks, and which sleeps. And what does the soul do? It reasons—it knows every one—it loves certain things, and dislikes others. Go on, in a playful manner, "Do you know this table?" *Yes.* "You know it then?" *To be sure.* "You see clearly that it is not made like that chair, which is formed of wood, and not like the chimney piece, of stone?" *Yes*, the child will reply. Proceed no farther without being convinced, by her tone of voice, and by the child's eyes, that these simple truths have struck her. Then say—But does this table know you? You will see that the child will begin laughing, and ridiculing, as it were, such a question.—No matter: go on—Which loves you the best, that table or that chair? She will still keep laughing—but pursue the discourse—Is the window very wise? Then try to go further—Does this doll answer you when you speak to it? *No.* Why—has it no intellect? *No, none.* It is not then like you; for you know it, and it does not know you. But after death, when you will be under the ground, shall not you be like this doll? *Yes.* You will no longer feel any thing? *No.* You will no longer know any body? *No.* And your soul will be in heaven? *Yes.* Will it not then see God? *True, it will.* And where is the soul of the doll at present? You will perceive that the child will answer with a laugh—or at least that it will make you understand the doll has no soul.

Upon this foundation, and by means of these simple illustrations, enforced at different times, you may accustom the child, by degrees, to attribute both to the body and the soul, that which is peculiar to each—provided you do not indiscreetly propose to her consideration, certain actions which are common to the one and the other. All subtilty must be avoided, as it perplexes truth; and we must content ourselves to point out, with care and correctness, those circumstances that mark distinctly the difference between the body and soul. Sometimes one meets with such stupid characters, whom even the help of a good education will not assist in the comprehension of these truths: however, they may be sometimes clearly *conceived,* without being perspicuously expressed. God sees better than we do into the spirit of man, what is there placed for the knowledge of his mysteries.

With respect to those children in whom we discover a mind capable of further researches, one may, without throwing them into a study which savours too much of philosophy, make them conceive, according to their inclination, what is meant when it is said that God is a spirit, and that the soul is also a spirit. I think that the best and most simple method of making them conceive this spirituality of God and of the soul, is, to make them remark the difference between a dead and living man: in the one, there is nothing but a body; in the other, the soul is united with the body. Afterwards you may shew them that that which is capable of reasoning, is more perfect than that which has mere form and motion. Then illustrate, by various examples, that no body perishes—that it is only separated: thus, pieces of burnt wood fall into charcoal, or evaporate in smoke. If then, you will add, that which is of itself only charcoal (incapable of knowing and thinking) perishes not—how much more shall the soul, which is capable of both knowledge and thought, endure for ever! The body may die—that is to say, may quit the soul and shrink into dust—but the soul will live; for it will always have the faculty of thinking.

Those who instruct children, should develop, as much as possible, these truths, which are the foundation of all religion. But if success should not crown their exertions, especially with dull obstinate children, let them hope that God will enlighten internally. There is, however, a sensible and practical way of confirming this knowledge of the distinction between body and soul—and that is, accustom children to despise the one, and regard the other, throughout their manners and intercourse with the world. Praise that instruction which nourishes the soul and causes it to expand: esteem those great truths which animate it to become wise and virtuous. Despise luxury of diet and dress, and every thing which enervates the body: make them sensible how much honour, a good conscience, and religion, are above these sensual pleasures. By the force of such sentiments, without reasoning upon the body and the soul, the ancient Romans taught their children to despise the body, and to sacrifise it to every thing which could inspire their minds with the pleasure of virtue and glory. With them, it was not simply persons of high birth, it was the entire mass of the people who lived temperately, disinterestedly, despising life, and sensible only of honour and wisdom, which excited their applause or imitation. When I speak of the ancient Romans, I mean those who lived before the extension of their empire had corrupted their simplicity of manners.

Let it not be said that children are incapable of receiving these prejudices from education. How often do we discover certain maxims which have been established among us, against the impression of our senses, by the force of custom alone. For instance, that of duelling—founded on a false principle of honour. It is not by reasoning, but by taking for granted, without reasoning, the maxim to be established on a principle of honour, that life is exposed, and that every man who carries a sword lives in continual danger. Those who have no quarrel may have one every moment with certain people, who are seeking every pretext to signalize themselves in some duel. However moderate one may be, such moderation is hardly preserved, without violating that false honour, which will not suffer you to avoid a quarrel by an explanation, or to refuse becoming the second of some one who has an inclination to fight. What authorities have not failed in eradicating so barbarous a custom! See, therefore, how powerful are the prejudices of education—But how much more powerful will they be on the side of virtue, supported by reason, and animated with the hope of happiness hereafter!

The Romans of whom we have been speaking, and before them the Greeks—in the good times of their republics, brought up their children in the contempt of luxury and effeminacy: they taught them to esteem glory—to be ardent, not to heap up riches, but to conquer those kings who possessed them—to believe that virtue alone was the road to happiness. This spirit was so strongly established in the foregoing republics, that they atchieved incredible things according to those maxims which were so contrary to the opinions of all other people. The examples of so many martyrs, and of other primitive christians of all conditions and ages, demonstrates that the grace of baptism being united with the help of education, may make impressions still more wonderful among the faithful, to enable them to despise every thing which is attached to the body. Seek then for every agreeable circumstance, every striking comparison, to convince children that our bodies are like the brutes—our souls like angels. Represent a knight mounted on a horse and directing its course: and say, that the soul is to the body, what the horseman is to the horse. Finish your remarks by observing that the soul is weak and miserable, when abandoned to the direction of the body; which, like a furious horse, would hurl it down a precipice. Relate, also, that the beauty of the body, or external person, is like a flower which blossoms in the morning, and withers and is trod under foot in the evening—but that the soul is the express image of the immortal beauty of God. There is, you may add, an order of things much more excellent, which cannot be seen by the gross eyes of the flesh—whereas every thing here below is subject to change and corruption. In order to make children sensible that there are really certain things, which neither the eyes nor the ears can apprehend, you may ask them whether it is not true that such a person is wise—and that such an one is witty or ingenious.—When they have answered *yes*, you may observe—"But have you *seen* the wisdom of such a person? Of what colour is it? Have you *heard* it? Does it make much noise? Have you *touched* it? Is it cold or hot?" The child will laugh: nevertheless put the same questions relating to wit or ingenuity.—She will appear quite astonished when she is asked of what colour is wit—whether it is round or square? Then you may make her remark that she knows there are many things in reality which she can neither see, touch, nor hear; and that these things are spiritual. But you must enter with great soberness and caution on these sort of conversations with girls. I only propose it here for the sake of those, whose curiosity and reason, will bring you, in spite of every effort to the contrary, to such questions. You must regulate the discourse according to the bias of the child's mind, and the necessity of the case.

Retain their understandings, as much as possible, within common limits: and teach them that there is a modesty with regard to science, which belongs to their sex, almost as delicate as that which is inspired by the horror of vice.

At the same time you must bring imagination to the aid of intellect; to give them pleasing images of the truths of religion, which the gross senses of the body are unable to behold. Paint to them the glory of heaven, such as St. John has represented it!—tears wiped away from every eye—neither death, disease, nor lamentation—all agonies ceasing, all evils at an end—eternal joy on the head of the righteous, like the waters on the head of a man immersed in the sea! Display that glorious Jerusalem, of which God himself will be the Sun, to create days without an end—a river of peace, a torrent of delight, a fountain of life, shall water it—there, every thing shall be gold, pearls, and precious stones.

I am well aware that all these images are attached to things sensible; but after having animated children with such a beautiful spectacle so as to rivet their attention, one may adopt the method just recommended to bring them to spiritual things.

Conclude, that we are, in this world, like travellers in an inn, or under a tent: that the body is hastening to decay, and that all our efforts can retard its corruption but a few years: but that the soul will fly away to that celestial country, where it will live for ever with God. If children can be brought to contemplate these grand objects with pleasure, and to judge of the common things of life through the medium of such high hopes, we shall have accomplished a most important task.

I would even try to impress them with strong ideas of the *resurrection of the body*. Teach them that nature is but the common order which God has established in his works, and that miracles are only exceptions to this common order; so that it is as easy for the Almighty to work an hundred miracles, as it is for me to go out of my room a quarter of an hour before my usual time of departure. Then call to recollection the history of the resurrection of Lazarus, of Jesus Christ, and of those apparitions which were recognised for forty days by a great number of persons. Next, shew that it cannot be difficult for that Being who created man, to bring him to life after dissolution; and do not forget the comparison of a grain of corn which is sowed in the earth, and decays, in order to reproduce and multiply its species.

Moreover, these moral lessons must not be taught children by memory, in like manner as they are taught the catechism: such a method would have an immediate tendency to convert religion into an affected language, or at least into troublesome formalities: only assist their understanding, and put them in the way of comprehending the foregoing truths on their proper foundations: they will, in consequence, appear more consistent and agreeable, and become more vividly impressed on the mind. Take advantage of every opportunity to make them develop with clearness, what they at present confusedly behold.

Always bear in mind that nothing will be more dangerous than to speak to them with contempt of this life, when, by the tenor of your conduct, they discover that you do not deliver your sentiments with sincerity and truth. In every period of life, example has an astonishing effect upon us—in infancy, it is every thing. Children are very fond of imitation; they have not yet acquired habits which render the imitation of another difficult—besides, not being of themselves able to judge profoundly of things, they judge much more from the example of those who propose, than from the reasons which they adduce in proposing, them. Actions are much more striking than words: so that if they observe your actions do not correspond with your precepts, they will be disposed to consider religion, only as a *specious ceremony*, and virtue as an *impracticable idea*.

Never indulge yourself before children, in any railleries about things which have relation to religion, or on the indiscretion of any pious persons: you may think all this innocent—you are mistaken—it will have its certain consequences. Never speak of God, or of what regards the worship of him, but with seriousness and respect, free from all levity—observe decorum in every thing, but particularly on this head. People who are very nice observers of it in what regards the world, are frequently gross and negligent in respect to religion.

When a child shall have made such necessary reflections as lead to a knowledge of herself and of God—add to them the historical facts in which she has already been instructed: this union will enable her to have a correct idea of the whole of religion: and she will remark with pleasure the connection between such reflections and the history of mankind. She will have observed that man did not make himself, that his soul is the image of God, that his body has been formed with so many admirable resources, by an industry and power which can only be divine—and she will then recollect the creation. Afterwards she will think that he is born with inclinations contrary to reason, that he has been deceived by pleasure, carried away by anger, and that his body hurries on his soul, contrary to reason, as a furious courser rushes forward with a horseman; instead, of the soul governing the body. She will perceive the cause of this disorder in the history of the sin of our first parents; and this history will lead her to that of the Saviour, who reconciles man to God. Such is the foundation of religion.

To make young people better understand the mysteries, actions, and precepts of Christ, we must dispose them to read the Evangelists. They must, therefore, be early prepared to read the word of God, as they are prepared to receive the holy communion of the Sacraments.[6]

Remember, then, to place before their eyes the Gospel, and the great examples of antiquity; but not till you are assured of their docility, and simplicity of faith. Provided you lay the foundation of humility, submission, and an aversion to all suspicious singularity, you will shew young people, with great benefit and effect, every thing the most perfect in the law of God, in the institution of the Sacrament, and in the practice of the ancient church. I know that one cannot hope to give these instructions, in their full latitude, to all sorts of children; I propose it only, in order that we may make use of them, as exactly as possible, according to circumstances, time, and the dispositions of them whom we instruct.

Superstition, without doubt, is to be avoided in the sex: but nothing eradicates or prevents it better than solid instruction: this instruction, although it ought to be restrained within proper bounds, and different from the studies of the learned, produces greater effects than is ordinarily imagined. A person sometimes thinks himself to be well informed, who in reality is not so; and whose ignorance is even so great that he is not in a condition to feel what he wants in order to know the foundation of christianity.

Never suffer any thing to be mixed with the faith, or the practices, of religion, that is not drawn from the Gospel. Carefully guard children against certain abuses which are but too common, and which are, therefore, too apt to be considered as points of present discipline in the church. These errors are not to be guarded against without recurring to the source, and knowing the origin of the usages and customs of holy men of the primitive ages. Children who are naturally too credulous, should never be used to admit *lightly* certain histories without authority; nor to attach themselves to certain devotions which are the offspring of an indiscreet zeal. The true way of in-

[6] Here follows, in the original, certain matter which may be thought to savour too strongly, on the one hand, of the authority due to the *Romish Church*; and on the other, of principles (resulting therefrom) which are now called *Evangelical*; and as such, contrary to the doctrine and tenets of the established Church of England.

structing them in these subjects, is, not to criticise those things which have often been introduced from pious notions, but to shew, without passing a severe censure, that they rest on no solid foundation. Content yourself with omitting these matters in your instructions relating to the christian religion: this silence will be sufficient, at first, to enable children to form a perfect idea of christianity, without adding practical cautions: In the course of your instructions, you may prepare them, by degrees, against the reasoning of *Calvinists*: I think this will not be useless, as we mingle every day with people prejudiced in favour of Calvinistical opinions, who deliver them in the most familiar conversations.

Give children a taste for plain, sensible, and edifying discourses—not for those that are full of vain and affected ornament: accustom their imaginations to hear death spoken of: to see, without perturbation, a funeral pall—an open grave—sick people who are dying, and those already dead: if you can do so without exposing them to violent emotions of fear.

Nothing is more to be lamented than to see many people, who are really religious, express a continued dread of death: some absolutely turn pale at finding the number *thirteen* at table—or on having had certain dreams—or having seen a saltseller thrown down: the fear arising from these imaginary presages is a gross remnant of paganism: make children see the folly and absurdity of them. Although women may not have the same opportunities of shewing their courage, as men, they ought nevertheless to possess it. Cowardice is despicable, every where, and has always bad effects. A woman should know how to resist vain alarms, and should be firm against unforeseen danger: let her cry and be agitated on great occasions only, and in them let virtue be her chief support. A christian of either sex should never be a coward. The soul of a christian, if one may so express it, is the contempt of this life, and the love of that which is to come.

Chapter VIII.

On Religious Studies.[7]

The preceding observations have sufficiently convinced us of the importance of religion, both as it affects our temporal and eternal welfare. It now follows that we instruct our children in the reading of certain religious works, which are not only considered to contain wholesome doctrine, but which may strengthen us in the opinions we have cherished, and establish, on an unshaken basis, "the reason of the hope that is in us."

Without a pretty accurate information of those *data*, on which our religion is formed, we become subject to the caprice or violence of certain artful characters, who seldom fail to perplex us, and undermine many of the essential articles of the christian faith; and who ultimately leave us, after pulling down the fair fabric we had built, in all the misery of doubt and distraction. The scriptures may be said to be written with the finger of God, on adamant which can never perish: it is not in the power of man to shake their authority, or to divert their proper influence on a sincere and pious mind. It is our duty to be careful to comprehend them thoroughly, to have as clear a conception as possible of their more mysterious parts, without harassing our minds if some things still remain for future revelation. We are not to censure what we do not, at first, understand: reason and knowledge are progressive—by degrees, the mist of ignorance is cleared away, and the sunshine of intelligence succeeds. Above all, let us not presumptuously conclude certain passages to be irrecoverably obscure, without consulting the many able commentators who have treated on them; but as the library of

[7] The present original chapter is substituted for that of Fenelon, as being more applicable, in the opinion of the translator, to the generality of female readers; at least to those of his own country.

a mother may not be extensively theological, let us apply for information to those pious pastors, and studious men, who have made these commentators their particular study. If we are so eager to satisfy ourselves and our children on the trifling topics that ordinary conversation gives rise to, how much more anxious should we be to obtain certainty and truth on the important doctrines of revelation!

I do not, however, mean that a child is to be always reading the bible, or sermons, or the catechism—nothing is so injudicious. At her tender years she can comprehend little of the doctrinal points of scripture; and besides, from such constant habits of perusing religious books, she may become fatigued and disgusted, and turn an indifferent ear to all future application to them. Let us avoid making children affectedly knowing in those subjects which sometimes require the mature years and profound study of divines to comprehend. Nothing is so disgusting as *cant*; as religious quotations in young people, who cannot, from their years and habits, have formed an accurate idea either of the meaning or application of what they quote: such things savour strongly of those *suspicious singularities* which Fenelon is so anxious to eradicate. The habit of quoting scripture in young persons of either sex, carries with it a pertness and conceit, which all judicious parents will be careful to discourage. Sacred truths, or religious denunciations, are not to be enforced by the levity of youth; ignorance and hypocrisy may be suspected where such premature sanctity prevails. If there be one thing more than another, which destroys the simplicity and harmless cheerfulness of girls, it is the giving them notions of puritannical gravity, and artificial sobriety of behaviour: joy and elasticity of spirits are not of themselves criminal. If we repress these innocent ebullitions, by inculcating formality and fastidiousness, we do as much mischief to the growth of the mind, as we should do to that of an upright and proportionate body, by the application of bandages and ligatures.

No small degree of care and skill is requisite for the direction of religious studies in young people, and especially in females; because the opposite sex, which is always fond of triumph, will be exerting every art, and trying every expedient, to weaken and subvert their arguments. If reason or superior knowledge fail, ridicule is resorted to; and this, it must be confessed, has a very strong effect on those young people of a disposition above described. In early years, religious impressions should be kept solemnly within the breast: they should be our consolation in affliction, our hope in distress, and the grand stimulus to prayer and meditation. It is well known, that from a premature disclosure of crude religious sentiments, ridicule and disgust are excited; and many an amiable and pious girl has suffered her principles to be shaken, and her faith to be overturned, by the buffoonery and sarcasm of a weak and contemptible antagonist. Let us endeavour to guard against this; and to prevent any ill effects arising from those important studies, which should be the ornament and solace of our lives.

From no quarter can a child receive religious instruction with more benefit than from a *mother*; and in proportion to the ignorance or indiscretion of the latter, will be that of the former. If a child is unaccustomed to see books of religion in her mother's library, she can have but little curiosity to peruse them; and if they at last be obtruded on her, she will naturally suspect the sincerity of her instructor, who produces works which she deems of the highest importance to her pupil's welfare, but of which she herself does not possess a single copy. This evil is easily remedied, if parents would only consider the importance of religious education; if, instead of crowding their shelves with the flimsy productions of novelists and romancers, they would admit a few judicious works, which treat of the evidences of the Christian religion, and describe the chief doctrines by which it is upheld. A portion of these studies might be given at stated times, or as the inclination of the child prompts, so as not to make them too formal or severe.

By the blessing of providence, we have, in our own country, a great abundance of excellent religious tracts, which display the rise, progress and establishment of the Christian religion. Men of eminence and piety—archbishops, bishops, divines of every rank, and laymen, have all contributed their talents, with various ability and success, to set forth the glory of the gospel, and the truths of the kingdom of heaven. Let us, therefore, attend to the doctrines which these wise and virtuous men, who have passed a long and studious life, as labourers in the vineyard of Christ, have illustrated and enforced. Let us not indulge chimeras and conceits of our own; but, with a diffidence and timidity, listen to those opinions of the learned and the good, whose abilities and opportunities have best entitled them to pronounce judgment. Nothing should be so much avoided as hasty and obstinate conclusions, drawn from premises which are not sufficiently understood.

In proportion to the breadth and depth of the foundation, will be the strength of the superstructure; and if we take care to place in the hands of young religious pupils, such sound and serious books as awaken piety, without kindling enthusiasm—as lead and satisfy the reason, without exciting vain and sceptical curiosity—as strengthen the mind, and meliorate the heart, without creating vanity, selfishness, and hypocrisy—we shall, I ardently conceive, have effected *that* which it was our wish and duty to perform.

Agreeably to these principles and reflections, I am desirous of recommending such plain, perspicuous, and sound works, as comprehend every thing relating to the elements, doctrines, and practice of christianity; and such as may not be difficult, or attended with great expence, in the procuring.

1. The Ten Commandments; *and the 5th, 6th, and 7th Chapters of the Gospel, according to St. Matthew*. These important parts of holy writ contain a fund of the most excellent and essential doctrines for a christian to know and practice; the primitive christians used to commit them to memory, and instruct their children in the application of them.[8]

2. Dr. Doddridge's *Three Sermons on the Evidences of Christianity*, separately published, from the particular superintendance and recommendation of the present Bishop of London. It is an useful tract, and is sold very cheap.

3. The (present) Bishop of London's *Summary of the Evidences of Christianity, &c.* which may be considered one of the most useful, and perspicuous treatises extant; it is very cheap.

4. Mr. Addison's *Treatise on the same*. This (which should properly

[8] Perhaps it may be advisable to have them printed separately, in large striking letters, so as to be impressed stronger on the child's imagination.

The following production may be worth obtaining; "An Abstract *of the Historical Part of the Old Testament, with References to other Parts of the Scripture, especially to the New Testament*;" which are placed at length in an opposite column. London: printed by W. Bowyer, 1730, 8vo. This is a very useful, though not generally known, publication. If it has not been reprinted, it is now probably scarce.

The work is "inscribed to the founders, benefactors, and trustees, of the charity schools." It was composed by that learned printer, Mr. Bowyer; and the introduction, written by way of preface, bears strong marks of the piety and talents of its author. It is followed by a "Translation of a Letter from the Earl of Mirandola and Concordia, to his nephew, then an officer in the army of the Emperor Charles V." This letter, which is too long to extract, is serious and impressive; and such as does great honour to the religious principles, and sound sense of the writer.

have been first noticed) is a beautiful and masterly dissertation, and worthy of the celebrity of its pious and elegant author.

5. GROTIUS *on the Truth of the Christian Religion.* Every enlightened mother will derive great pleasure and benefit from the perusal of this incomparable treatise. It has been translated by John Clark, and lately by the Rev. Mr. Madan, from the Latin of the famous Grotius. Students in divinity are usually examined in the original when they present themselves for holy orders.

6. BISHOP PRETTYMAN'S *Elements of Christian Theology*. This is a work of deserved repute, and will be found greatly instructive. The historical events of scripture are detailed in an interesting manner, and cannot fail to afford the most pleasing conviction of the truth of what is related. There has been an abridgment of it in one large 8vo. volume, by the Rev. Mr. Clapham. The original is in 2 vols. 8vo.

7. SECKER (Archbishop) *on the Catechism*: and WILSON (Bishop) *on the Sacrament.* These are truly excellent treatises: their established celebrity renders no further recital of them necessary in this place.

8. SERMONS: by *Dr. S. Clarke; Abp. Secker, Sherlock, Jortin, Balguy, Porteus*, (Bishop of London), *Blair*, and *Carr*.[9] These among many other excellent ones, whose enumeration would swell the list to an unnecessary size, may be perused and meditated on with great advantage. They are not selected in rejection of others, but solely as containing much sound and edifying matter, which may bring forth "sixty and an hundred fold."

9. WILSON'S (Bishop) *Bible, with Commentaries*: in 3 vols. 4to. Bath: printed by Crutwell. Perhaps, the most judicious and unexceptionable illustration of the sacred text extant.

10. GISBORNE'S *Duties of Women*, and *Familiar Survey of the Christian Religion*, are both very excellent performances, and reflect great credit on the head and heart of the distinguished and benevolent writer.

11. *The Whole Duty of Man.*

12. *The Ladies' Calling.* These two last works are from the same anon-

[9] Miss Boudler has published a small volume of useful sermons to a country congregation, which it may be advisable to procure. Her name is not prefixed to the work; but it is published by *Cadell* and *Davies*, in the Strand.

ymous author, whose publications are, indeed, purer than gold—"yea, than much fine gold."

Such are the works recommended to the perusal and meditation of serious and enlightened parents: and such, it is hoped, will not bring forth "bitter fruits."

There are moments of languor and heaviness, of dulness and despondency, to which the best of mothers may be exposed, and which may be removed, or relieved, by a perusal of some of the foregoing writers: in such moments, she will know the full value of their works, and will not repent the trouble or expence incurred in the procuring of them. She will then be convinced that the common productions, which amuse the ignorant and the foolish, could not have supplied the want of them; whether in soothing the pangs which arise from a deceased husband or child, or in teaching her to bear up with fortitude against the frowns of a persecuting world. The balm of consolation, which arises from these studies, she will pour into the bosom of a dutiful daughter; and the knowledge that she has gained by experience, will be imparted to, and grow up with, her rising posterity.

Let it always be impressed on our minds, that if we are so anxious to procure costly furniture, or splendid apparel, which the moth eats, or the thief steals, how much more is it our duty to devote a comparatively trifling sum towards the acquisition of those mental treasures, of which neither treachery nor violence can dispossess us, and which fit us, by degrees, for the eternal mansions of happiness and rest.

It has been observed, that the female sex is more liable to fanaticism than the male; the history, however, of religious sectaries, does not authorise this observation: instances of violence and mad persecution may be adduced, in which females have taken a very subordinate part, or indeed none at all; and while the examples of Athanasius and Arius are fresh in the memory, we need not resort to another. That the warmth and susceptibility of a female mind renders it exposed to strong impressions, before the judgment begins to operate, cannot be disputed. What pleases on the first impression is not easily eradicated; and we conclude that to be true, which flatters some previous opinion, or favour some secret bias. Error, thus introduced, is not extirpated without difficulty: and if to the pliancy and sensibility of a female mind, we add, that opportunities are seldom offered of going into deep critical investigations, or listening to opposite opinions, which are founded on reason and experience, it will not appear surprising that women are sometimes warm in their religious sentiments, and slow and reluctant to abandon them.

Hence follows the necessity of a *proper religious instruction*—of an adherence to those doctrines and opinions, which, on a careful survey of the many that have agitated mankind, seem to be the best calculated for ensuring our present and future welfare. In thus offering advice on so important a subject, the translator has ventured to advance certain sentiments, and to recommend certain works, which in his humble apprehension, appeared likely to be productive of some assistance and advantage. When he recommends a conformity to the tenets of the ESTABLISHED CHURCH OF THIS COUNTRY, he does so from a conscientious conviction of its purity and excellence; from a recollection of the many great and good men who have lived and died in its cause; and whose works remain a glorious monument of their diligence, piety, and learning. While reason, integrity, and virtue, have any influence on the human character, while practical good is acknowledged to be superior to plausible theory, so long shall the luminous and illustrious divines of the English Church rise above all the pretensions of fanatical and self-inspired teachers, who turn the word of God into craft, and use the name of Jesus with their lips, while their hearts are estranged from him.

That the foregoing sentiments may tend to promote true sober-minded religion—to adorn the female character with those charms which arise from the substance, and not the form, of piety—to excite cheerfulness without levity—seriousness without despondency—and happiness in this present state without groundless anxieties of the future—is the earnest and ardent wish of their author.

Chapter IX.

Remarks on Ordinary Defects among Girls.

We are now to speak of the care and attention which are requisite to preserve girls from many defects to which they are too commonly addicted. They are oftentimes brought up in so effeminate and timid a manner, as to be rendered incapable of a firm and regular conduct. At first there is much affectation, which afterwards become habitual, in those ill-founded fears, and in those tears, which are so cheaply and plentifully bestowed. A contempt of such affectations would operate greatly in correcting them; as they are in a considerable degree the offspring of vanity.

They should also be repressed in the indulgence of too violent friendships, little jealousies, excessive compliments, and flatteries: all these things spoil them, and accustom them to imagine that dryness and austerity belongs to every thing which is serious and grave. We should strive to effect this, so that their common mode of parlance be short and precise. A good understanding consists in retrenching all superfluous discourse, and in saying much in few words: whereas, the greater part of women say little in many words. They mistake facility of utterance and vivacity of imagination for good sense: they make no selection of their thoughts: they observe no order in regard to the things they have to explain: they are passionate in every thing they utter, and passion produces loquacity. Nothing very excellent can be expected of a woman, if she is not obliged to reflect on consequences, to examine her thoughts, to explain them in a precise manner, and afterwards to be silent.

Another circumstance which greatly contributes to the loquacity of women, is, that they are naturally artificial, and use a *roundabout* manner to arrive at the proper end. They are fond of *finesse*: and how is it possible they should be otherwise, when they are ignorant of a more prudent method—and when it is usually the first thing which example has taught them? They have a soft and ductile nature which enables them easily to play a part in every thing: tears cost them nothing: their passions are lively, and their knowledge limited: hence it is that they neglect nothing to come off successful—and that they admire certain methods, which to a serious and prudent woman would appear very exceptionable: they seldom stop to enquire whether such a thing is desirable, but are anxious and indefatigable only in obtaining it. Add to this, they are timid and full of what is called "*mauvais honte*;" which is another source of dissimulation. The method of preventing so great an evil, never to put them under a necessity of finessing, but accustom them to declare ingenuously their sentiments upon every lawful topic. Let them be at liberty to express their *ennui* whenever they feel it: and let them never be subjected to feign an admiration of certain persons or certain books, which in reality displease them.

Sometimes a mother is prejudiced against a governess, and undertakes the management of the child herself, while the daughter cunningly acts contrary to her taste. When children are so wretched that they are under the necessity of disguising their sentiments, the way of extricating them from such a dilemma, is, to instruct them solidly in the maxims of true prudence—as one perceives that the method of correcting a taste for novels and romances, is, by exciting a turn for useful and agreeable histories. If you do not encourage a rational curiosity, they will entertain an irrational one—in like manner, if you do not form their minds on the principles of true prudence, they will become attached to falsehood, which is, in fact, *finesse*.

Shew them, by examples, how one is able, without duplicity, to be discreet, foresighted, and attached to *legitimate* means of succeeding. Tell them that prudence consists chiefly in speaking little—in entertaining a greater distrust of oneself than of others, and not in uttering false sentiments, and playing a deceitful part. An upright conduct, and a general reputation for integrity, begets more confidence and esteem, and, in the end, even more temporal advantages, than perverse and suspicious habits. How much does this judicious rectitude of conduct distinguish a person, and render her fit for the most important undertakings!

But add, how base and contemptible is *premeditated finesse*! it is either an account of some trifle which one is ashamed to mention, or it must be considered as a pernicious passion. When one wishes for that which it is lawful to wish for, the request is made openly—and it is sought for in a direct and proper method, with moderation. What is there more delightful and agreeable, than to be sincere? always tranquil—always content—having nothing to fear or to feign? On the contrary, a dissimulating character is always in agitation—remorse—and danger—and under the deplorable necessity of covering *one finesse* by substituting an *hundred others.*

With all these shameful disquietudes, artificial characters never escape that misery from which they are constantly flying—sooner or later their *real* character will appear. If the world has been their dupe in some single action, it will not continue so during the whole of their lives: oftentimes they are the dupes of those whom they wished to deceive: for there is sometimes an appearance of being dazzled by them, and they think themselves beloved—at the very moment, perhaps, when they are despised. At least they cannot prevent suspicion—and can any thing be more contrary to the rational interests of a prudent woman, than to see herself always suspected? Unfold these things by degrees—according as opportunity, necessity, or the bent of your pupil's intellect, may suggest.

Observe, however, that cunning (or *finesse*) is always the offspring of a base heart and narrow-minded spirit. In proportion as we wish to conceal our views we become cunning—being convinced that we are not as we ought to be—or, that, seeking for lawful objects, we adopt unworthy means of obtaining them—which arises from our ignorance in seeking such objects. Make children remark the impertinence of certain artifices that they see practised—the contempt which it draws on those practising them—and lastly, make them ashamed of themselves when you detect them in some dissimulation. As they grow up, deprive them of what they love, when they wish to obtain it by *artifice*—but declare, that they shall possess it when they ask *openly*: do not be afraid even of indulging their little weaknesses, in order to give them an opportunity and the courage of shewing them. False shame is the most dangerous of evils and the most difficult to cure; and this too, if great care be not taken, will render all others irremediable.

Paint, in their proper colours, those infamous artifices by which they would wish to deceive their neighbour without having the reproach of deceiving him: there is more perfidy and knavery in these refinements, than in common artifices. Some people, one may say, boldly practice deception—but wretches of the preceding description, add novelty and disguise to authorise it. Tell a child that God *is truth itself*—that it is mocking *him* when we jest at truth in our discourse—which should be precise and correct, and should consist in few words, that truth be not violated.

Be on your guard not to imitate those who applaud children, when they have discovered sharpness of intellect by some *finesse*. Far from supposing these tricks pretty and diverting, check them severely—and manage it so, that all their artifice may end unsuccessfully, and experience at last may disgust them with it. In praising them for such and such faults, we, in fact, persuade them that *ability* and *deception* are one and the same thing.

Chapter X.

The Vanity of Beauty and Dress.

Nothing is more to be dreaded among young girls, than *vanity*—as they are born with a violent desire to please. Those roads which conduct *men* to authority and fame being shut to *them*; they strive to be recompensed by the charms of intellect and person: hence flows their conversation so soft and so insinuating—hence it is that they aspire, as well to beauty, as to all the exterior graces, and become passionately fond of dress. A turban or bandeau is of the greatest importance in their estimation.

This excess is carried farther in our country[10] than in any other. That volatile disposition so remarkable among us, causes a continual variety of fashions: so that, to the love of dress is added the love of novelty, which has strange charms for some people. These two follies united, reverses all orders and conditions, and corrupts all manners. As soon as *certain rules* are done away in respect to our clothes and furniture, the same irregularity prevails in our conditions. Public authority cannot settle a "table of particulars:"[11] every one, therefore, chooses according to his money; or rather, without money, according to his ambition and vanity.

This passion for splendor ruins families; and the ruin of families brings with it a corruption of manners. On the one hand, it begets, in persons of mean extraction, a passion for a large fortune (which religion assures us is sinful); on the other, among people of quality who find their resources

[10] France.

[11] This is construed in the above manner in preference to "the table of particular persons:" conceiving that Fenelon means "certain rules or laws" to be observed in regard to *living* and *dressing*. *T.*

exhausted, it produces mean and dirty practices in order to support their extravagance: hence, honor, fidelity, integrity, and benevolence, (even towards their nearest relatives,) are extinguished for ever!

These evils arise from the influence of vain women in directing the fashions; they ridicule those, as antiquated dames, who wish to preserve the gravity and simplicity of ancient manners.

Be particularly zealous, therefore, to make girls understand how much more estimable is that honor which flows from an upright conduct and sound capacity, than that which arises from the elegance and splendor of dress. Beauty, you may say, deceives the possessor of it much more than it does those whom it dazzles: it agitates and intoxicates the soul; we are more foolishly idolising ourselves, than the most passionate lovers the object of their affection. A few years only make the difference between a beautiful and ordinary woman. Beauty is not desirable unless it produces advantageous marriages: and how should it effect this, unsupported by merit and virtue? A girl, merely beautiful, can only hope to be united to a giddy young man, with whom she is pretty certain of misery: on the contrary, her good sense and modesty would cause her to be sought for by prudent men, sensible of such solid qualifications. Those whose fame consists only in their beauty, soon become ridiculous: they approach, without perceiving it, to a certain age in which their charms begin to fade; still, however, indulging the dear delusion of self-gratification, when the world has long ago been disgusted with their vanity. In short, it is as unreasonable to be attached *solely to beauty*, as to concentrate all merit in strength of body; a maxim, which barbarians and savages only inculcate.

From beauty let us pass to DRESS. True grace does not depend on a vain and affected exterior; although propriety, and some little skill may be shewn in our necessary clothing. But after all, these silks or satins, which may be pretty enough, can never be considered as ornaments which *confer* beauty.

I would even make young girls remark that noble simplicity which appears in the drapery of *statues*, and in many figures which yet remain of Grecian and Roman *costume*. They should contemplate the superiority of hair negligently tied behind, and of the broad folds of a full and floating drapery. It would also be as well for them to hear painters and connoisseurs, who possess a true taste for the antique, converse on these subjects.

In proportion as their understanding rose superior to the prejudices of fashion, they would hold in contempt those artificial modes of twisting and curling the hair, and all the paraphernalia of a fashionable woman. I am aware that one should not wish them to assume an entirely-antique costume of dress, which would be extravagant, and sometimes indecent: but they might, without the affectation of singularity, model their taste on that simplicity of attire, which is so noble, so delightful, and in all respects conformable to the manners of christians. Make them observe often, and by times, the vanity and, frivolousness of that mind which is sacrificed to the inconstancy of fashion.[12] True grace follows, but never does violence to, nature.

Fashion, however, soon destroys itself: it is perpetually aiming at perfection, and never finds it; at least, it never stops when it *has* found it. It would be reasonable enough if all changing and alteration were to cease after having found perfection, comprising both elegance and utility: but to change for the sake of changing, appears very much like sacrificing true politeness and good taste to inconstancy and confusion! Fashions are frequently founded on mere caprice. Women are the sole arbitrators of them; and it being difficult to say, who is to be believed or imitated, the most giddy and least informed seduce and influence the rest. They neither choose nor leave any thing according to rule: it is quite sufficient if one thing, though useful, has been long adopted: it ought to be discarded: and another thing, though perfectly ridiculous, but having the charm of novelty, is immediately substituted in its place, and becomes the admiration of all. After having laid a proper foundation, describe to them the rules of *christian modesty*. We learn, you will say, that man is born in the corruption of sin: his body, exposed to a contagious malady, is an inexhaustible source of temptation to his soul. Our Saviour has taught us to place all our virtue in fear and distrust of ourselves. Would you, we may exclaim, hazard your own soul and that of your neighbour by the indulgence of a foolish vanity? Look, therefore, with horror upon the exposure of the bosom and all other indecencies! When these absurdities are even committed without any premeditated passion, they, at least, savour strongly of vanity, and betray an unbridled desire to please. Does this variety justify, before God and man, so rash and scandalous a conduct, and so likely to be imitated by others? This

[12] A preceding and subsequent sentence in the original is here omitted; because it has an allusion to antiquated *high head dresses*; which are now, I believe, banished not only from France, but from Europe. The present simple and unaffected mode of female dress, (with some ridiculous and indelicate exceptions) is in general very conformable to the taste and advice of Fenelon.

blind passion of pleasing, is it conformable to a christian character, which should consider every thing as idolatrous, that perverts the love of God, and kindles the contempt of his creatures? When such giddy female characters strive to please—what is their real object? Is it not to excite the passions of men? And can they regulate these passions when in their possession? If women go too far, ought they not to be answerable for the consequences? And do they not always go too far, when their minds have been but little enlightened? You are absolutely preparing a subtile and deadly poison, and pouring it on the spectators beneath, and yet you imagine yourself *innocent*! When you address your pupils in this strong manner, add to it, the example of those whom modesty has recommended, and those whom indelicacy has covered with dishonor. Above every thing, never suffer children's minds to be filled with ideas that suit not with their condition. Repress severely all their whims and fantasies—shew them the inevitable danger which follows—and how much they make themselves despised by wise and discreet people, in thus assuming a character which does not belong to them.

What now remains to be effected, is, the managing of children of high and animated spirit. If care be not taken of this, when they have any vivacity, they intrigue: they wish to speak on every topic: they decide on works the least calculated for their capacity, and affect, through extreme delicacy, to be easily fatigued and overpowered. A girl should never speak but when necessity prompts: and then, with an air of deference and doubt: they should never even discuss subjects above the level of a common understanding, how well soever versed in them. Let a child possess a good memory and vivacity—shew pleasant little turns, and a facility of *graceful* eloquence—all these qualifications she may have in common with a great number of other stupid and contemptible women. But an exact and uniform conduct—an equal and regulated spirit—when to be silent, and when to speak—these rare qualifications will indeed distinguish her among her sex. As to squeamish delicacy and affectation of *ennui*, she must be repressed in both—by shewing her that a correct taste and good understanding consist in accommodating oneself to every thing in proportion to its utility.

Good sense and virtue are alone estimable. These will teach her to consider disgust and *ennui*, not as a commendable delicacy, but as the weakness of a diseased mind.

Since one must sometimes associate with gross characters, and mingle in occupations not altogether congenial—reason, which is the only real delicacy to be indulged, should instruct us to accommodate ourselves according to every emergency. An understanding which knows in what true politeness consists, and practises it, but which aspires to objects beyond it, in the hope of enjoying more solid attainments—is infinitely superior to delicate and merely polite characters, who are subject to be disgusted by their own nicety and refined taste.

Chapter XI.

Instruction of Women in their Duties.

Let us now discuss, in detail, those particulars of which it is the duty of a woman to be well informed. What are her employments? She is charged with the education of her children—of the boys, till a certain age—of the girls till they are married; of the conduct, manners, and morals of her domestic attendants; of the whole detail of household expenses; of the means of managing every thing with credit and economy; and sometimes, of the regulation of farms and the receipt of profits which arise from them.

Women, as well as men, should adapt their pursuits in literature and science to their situations and functions in life; and according to their occupations, should be their studies. We must, therefore, confine the instruction of women to the foregoing circumstances. But a curious woman, wishing to pry into every thing, may fancy that these instructions will confine her curiosity within narrow limits indeed—she is mistaken, because she knows not the importance and extent of the particulars in which I wish her to be instructed.

What discernment is necessary to know the disposition and genius of each of her children! to find out the proper mode of conduct so as to discover their humours, inclinations, and talents! to check those passions which are born with them, to inculcate good maxims, and to cure them of their errors! What prudence should she possess, to acquire and preserve authority over them, without forfeiting their confidence and esteem! Has she not also need of observing and thoroughly knowing those people whom she places near them? Undoubtedly she has: a mother of a family ought to be completely instructed in religion, and to possess a mature firm mind, adapted to, and experienced in, the government of her children.

Can it be supposed that women ought *not* to be explicitly and *formally instructed* in these duties, because they naturally fall into them during the lives of their husbands, who are generally engaged in business from home? Or, if widows, they still attend to them more closely? St. Paul generally attaches the salvation of mothers to the good education of daughters; for by these, he assures them, they will be saved.

I do not here take upon me to explain all that a woman ought to know for the education of her daughters; because such a memorial would make them sufficiently feel the extent of that knowledge which it is their duty to obtain.

To the government of families, add ECONOMY. The greater part of women neglect it as a mean consideration, fit only for country folks or farmers; or, at best, for innkeepers and housekeepers. Women nursed in the lap of affluence, luxury, and idleness, not only neglect, but despise, this domestic virtue; and seem to be forgetful of a middle state between the rusticity of a peasant, and the wildness of a Canadian savage. If you speak to them of the sale of corn, of the cultivation of lands, of the different kinds of revenue, of the receipt or raising of rents and other seignoral rights, of the best method of laying out farms, and appointing receivers, they imagine that you wish to reduce them to occupations, unworthy of their rank and character.

Ignorance is the offspring of their contempt for economy. The ancient Greeks and Romans, so distinguished for their ability and politeness, studied economy with the utmost care: some of their finest writers, from their own experience, have composed works which we still possess, and in which they give an account of the latest improvements of agriculture. It is well known that even their conquerors did not disdain to work in the field; and instances have come down to us in which the splendor of a triumph was followed by the care and conduct of a plough. All this is so foreign to our own customs and manners, that we should not credit it if it were not supported by historical truth. But is it not natural that the defence or augmentation of a country should be subordinate to the ultimate object of cultivating it peaceably? Of what advantage is victory, if it enable us not to gather the fruits of peace? After all, solidity of intellect consists in wishing to be exactly informed of the way in which those things operate, which constitute the foundations of human life: the greatest occurrences are regulated by this principle. The strength and felicity of a country consists not in the possession of provinces badly cultivated, but in the enjoyment of those productions of the earth which are necessary and sufficient for the sustenance of a numerous people.

Without doubt it requires a more elevated and comprehensive genius to be instructed and well informed in all the particulars relating to economy, and to be thereby able to regulate an entire family (which is a little republic), than to play, talk of the fashions, and be expert in all the little polite arts of conversation. That is a contemptible mind indeed, which aspires not beyond perfection in the talent of conversation: one sees, on all sides, women whose discourse is full of sound sense and solid maxims—while this conduct is replete with frivolousness and absurdity—the effect of not applying by times to better pursuits.

But take care of the opposite defect: women run a risk of being in extremes in every thing. It would be advisable for them, from their infancy, to have the management of some trifling affair—to keep accounts—to see the mode of bargaining for what they purchase, and to know how each thing should be made to answer a good use. Take care, also, that economy borders not on avarice: shew them, in detail, all the absurdities attendant on this latter passion. Tell them that "avarice gains little, and dishonors itself greatly." A reasonable mind will seek, in a frugal and laborious life, only how to avoid the shame and injustice attached to a prodigal and ruinous conduct. Superfluous expenses are to be retrenched as they enable a person to devote a portion of money to satisfy the claims of benevolence, friendship, and charity: great gain is frequently the result of seasonable forbearance: good order and management, and not sordid savings, are the source of profit. Do not fail to expose the gross error of those female economists who pertinaceously forbid a mold candle, while they suffer their whole affairs to be subjected to the knavery or rapacity of a steward. Respect propriety as well as economy. Accustom young people to do nothing in a slovenly and disorderly manner, and to remark the least disarrangement in a house. Make them also sensible that nothing so much contributes to propriety and economy, as the keeping of every thing in its proper place. This rule appears too trifling to mention; nevertheless it goes a great way if it be rigidly observed. For instance—are you in want of any thing? not a moment is lost in finding it—there is neither trouble, disputation, nor embarrassment attending its search: you put your hand immediately upon it, and when satisfied, replace it in the situation where you found it. This *nice order* constitutes one of the essential parts of propriety; and every eye is struck with the neat appearance of so exact an arrangement. Moreover, a particular place allotted to each article, not only has a pleasing appearance, but, in reality, tends to the preservation of that article. It is *used* less than it otherwise would be—it is not so frequently spoilt by accident—it is even more respected and treasured: for example, a vase would never be covered with dust, or become liable to be broken, if it were instantly put away after being done with. A passion for arranging things orderly, produces a love of neatness; and this will appear very advantageous, if it be considered that by such means servants are never encouraged in idleness and confusion. Again, something is gained by making their service prompt and easy, and depriving us of an opportunity of becoming impatient and impetuous, which is generally the case when things cannot be found from confusion and irregularity.

At the same time, avoid the excess of politeness and propriety. When propriety is within moderation, it is a virtue; but when we consult too much our own tastes and fancies, it is converted into a littleness of mind. Good taste rejects excessive delicacy: it treats little matters *as* little ones, and is not hurt at any unpleasant consequences resulting therefrom. Ridicule, before children, those knick-knacks and gewgaws, of which some women are prodigiously fond, and which lead them insensibly into unwarrantable expenses. Accustom young people to a propriety and decorum which is simple and easy of practice—shew them the best way of managing things—but shew them also the advantage of slighting them. Tell them how paltry and contemptible it is to grumble if a dish be badly seasoned, if a curtain be unevenly folded, or a chair be too high or too low.

It is undoubtedly better to be naturally coarse, than to have an overweening delicacy in matters of little moment. This pernicious delicacy, if not repressed in women of understanding, is more dangerous as it regards conversation than every thing else: to females of this stamp, the greater part of mankind appears insipid or fatiguing: the least deviation from politeness is monstrous: and they are always ridiculing and disgusted. Make such women know betimes that nothing is so injudicious as judging superficially of people by their manners, instead of examining the very bottom of their intellect, their sentiments and useful qualities. Convince them, by a variety of proofs, how much a country woman, with a coarse or even ridiculous manner, but with a good heart and sound understanding, is more estimable than a courtisan, who, under an acquired politeness, hides an ungrateful and unjust heart, capable of every meanness and dissimulation. Observe also, that those characters are always weak which incline to idleness and disgust. There is no one whose conversation is so bad, as that some good may not, occasionally, be drawn from it; and although a person at liberty would prefer choosing the best characters to converse with, yet there is some consolation, when reduced to converse with inferior characters, that we may make them talk on subjects that they understand, from which, perhaps, some information may be gained. But let us now return to those particulars in which a girl should be instructed.

Chapter XII.

Continuation of the Duties of Women.

To the duties previously enumerated, may be added the art of *choosing and retaining servants*. We should employ such as have honor and religion: their offices should be distinctly ascertained: the time and trouble which each thing requires, the manner of doing it well, and the expense attending it, should also be considered. It would be absurd (for instance) to find fault with a servant if you wished her to dress any thing quicker than it could be dressed; and if you have not some knowledge of the quantity and price of the ingredients which compose dishes, you will be liable to become the dupe or the scourge of your domestics; so that a knowledge of these matters is essential to a mistress of a family.

It is also necessary to know their humours, to manage their tempers, and to regulate in a christian-like manner this little household republic, which is, in general, sufficiently turbulent. Authority, is absolutely essential in this respect; for the more unreasonable servants are, the more they should be made obedient by fear: but as they are your brethren in Christ, and members of his kingdom, a rigid authority should never be exercised towards them, unless previous persuasion is found to fail.

Strive, therefore, to be beloved by your servants, without descending to low familiarity; enter not into conversation with them, but at the same time do not be backward in occasionally speaking, with kindness and affability, respecting their wants and concerns; and let them be assured of finding in you a compassionate counsellor. Do not check them too eagerly in their faults—appear neither surprised nor dissatisfied, provided you think them not incorrigible: let them gently hear reason; and submit frequently to little losses by their service, that you may be able coolly to convince them, that it is not from impetuosity and chagrin that you correct them, but rather for their own, than your, interest.

It would be no easy task to accustom *young women of fashion* to adopt a conduct, at once so amiable and benevolent. The impatience and ardor of youth, united with the false idea they are apt to entertain of their birth, often induce them to treat their domestics pretty nearly the same as they do their horses—they imagine that servants are any thing but what they really are—and made solely for the convenience of their masters. Endeavour to shew how revolting these principles are to modesty in yourself, and to humanity towards your neighbour.

Let it be comprehended that men are not born to be slaves—that it is a brutal error to suppose our fellow mortals are created to flatter our laziness and pride; that servitude being established against the natural equality of mankind, we should endeavour to soften it as much as possible; that masters themselves, though above their servants in situation, are not free from errors, and therefore should not expect an exemption from them in domestics; especially as they have not had the benefit of instruction and good example—and lastly, if servants become good for nothing by serving ill, masters also, frequently, become so, by being served well: for a facility of accommodation in every wish, and an immediate gratification in every desire, only softens and effeminates the soul, and renders it peevish and irritable under every trifling inconvenience.

Nothing is so well calculated to effect this domestic government, as the being *early* initiated in it. Give a young woman something to manage herself, on condition of her rendering you some account of it: this confidence will delight her, for youth is highly pleased when it is thought worthy of confidence, and capable of doing serious business. The example of Queen Margaret is a fine illustration of this. That princess informs us, in her memoirs, that the most sensible pleasure she ever experienced, was in seeing the queen, her mother, begin to converse with her, when she was very young, as with a person of years and maturity—she felt transported with joy on entering into the secrets of state with the queen and her brother the Duke of Anjou, reflecting that, not long ago, she had been immersed in the pastimes of children. Overlook the faults of a child in her first attempts at these things, and sacrifice something in order that she may ultimately gain instruction. Make her sensible, in a mild manner, of what she should have said or done, to avoid the inconveniencies into which she has been betrayed. Relate to her what has happened to yourself, and be not anxious to suppress faults, similar to her own, which you committed when young. Thus will you inspire her with confidence; without which, all education is but a formal wearisome task.

Teach a girl to read and write correctly. It is a shameful thing, but too common, to see women of understanding and good breeding, who cannot accurately pronounce what they read: either they stammer, or have a sort of singing or whine in their reading—whereas good reading consists in a simple and natural, but firm and even, tone of voice. They are, moreover, sometimes grossly deficient in orthography; either as to the manner of forming, or connecting, their letters when writing: at any rate they should be taught to write straight, and in a character neat and legible.

A girl should know the grammar of her own language; not, however, that she is to be taught by rule, as schoolboys are taught the Latin language—but that she be used to distinguish the different tenses, in an obvious and easy manner; to make use of proper terms; and to explain their thoughts, in a way, at once clear and concise. By these means you will enable her one day to teach her own children to speak accurately without previous study. It is well known that in ancient Rome, the mother of the Gracchi contributed greatly, by a sound education, to improve the language of her children, who became afterwards such eminent characters.

Females should also be instructed in the first four rules of arithmetic; namely, in addition, subtraction, multiplication, and division; which will be of essential use to them in keeping accounts. This, though a very important, is a very disagreeable, occupation with many people; but early habits, joined to a facility of quick reckoning, by the help of rules, will overcome every antipathy, and enable us to arrange the most perplexed accounts. No one can be ignorant that a correct method of keeping them is often productive of good order throughout an establishment.

It will be prudent also to give them a knowledge of the principal rules of justice: for example, of the difference between a gift and a thing bequeathed; between a contract, an entail, and a copartnership of inheritance; the general rules of law, or the particular customs of a country, which render these things valid; what is exclusive, and what is common, property; what goods are moveable, and what immoveable. When women marry, they will find a knowledge of these things of great importance to them.

But, at the same time, convince them, how incapable they are of entering deeply into the subtilties of law: how much the law itself, by the weakness of human reason, is subject to obscurity, and doubtful rules: how it varies: how uncertain every thing is that depends upon judicial decision, clear and upright as it may seem: how ruinous and insupportable is the law's delay, even in the most obvious cases.[13]

All this is of importance for women to know, in order to abate their fondness for lawsuits, and to prevent their trusting implicitly to counsellors, who would dissuade them from peaceful measures. When they are widows, or mistresses of their estates in any other way, they may do well to hear their agents, but not blindly follow them. They should act with the utmost caution in any suits their agents may advise them to undertake; and consult men of greater ability, and such as are more inclined to recommend the advantages of compromise: in short they should be assured, that the best ability in law causes, is, to foresee the mischiefs of them, and to know how they may be avoided.

Young women of rank and large fortune should be acquainted with the duties more particularly attached to great estates: tell them therefore, what should be done, to prevent the abuses, violence, tricks and treacheries so common in the country; how they ought to establish little schools and charitable societies, for the relief of the sick and needy: shew them also the handicraft trades, that may be set on foot in certain countries, to help the poor; and above all, how they may be taught useful knowledge and christian conduct; this however will lead to a detail too long to be here discussed.

[14]These instructions having been attended to, I think it may not be improper to allow young women, according to their leisure and capacity, the perusal of profane or classical writers, provided there be nothing in them to inflame or mislead the passions: these will be a means also of giving them a distaste for plays and romances. Put into their hands, therefore, the Greek and Roman historians; they will there see prodigies of courage and disin-

[13] I have here omitted two or three passages of the original, because they describe such incongruity and perniciousness in the law of France, as cannot be applicable to the modes observed in the British courts of judicature. *T.*

[14] Another passage of the original is also here omitted; because it relates to the observance of certain feudal rites, and to a knowledge of real property, which can be of no service to a woman in this country. *T.*

terestedness: let them be acquainted likewise with the history of their *own country*, which has its excellencies also, and with that of the neighbouring or foreign countries, judiciously written. All this will serve to enlarge their understandings, and to fill their hearts with noble sentiments, provided you guard against vanity and affectation. It is generally thought a necessary part of a good education, for a young lady of rank to be taught the Italian and Spanish languages: for my part I see no use in these acquirements, unless the lady is to be connected with some Spanish or Italian princess:[15] besides these two languages often lead them to books that are dangerous, and which might increase the faults to which they are liable; there is much to lose, and little to be gained, by these studies. Latin might be of some use; even in cultivating the elegancies of language, they will find the Latin more perfect than the Italian and Spanish, which are full of quaint conceits, and a wantonness of imagination bordering on extravagance: Latin however should be taught to young women of good judgment and discreet conduct only; who will set no greater value on this study than it deserves; who will renounce all vain curiosity, and have no other view than their own edification.

I would allow also, but with great care, the perusal of works of eloquence and poetry, if I saw they had a taste for them, and solidity of judgment enough to confine themselves to their real use: but fearful of agitating too much their lively imaginations, I would have the utmost caution observed in this respect: every thing that may awaken the sentiments of love, seems to me the more dangerous in proportion as it is softened and disguised.

Music and Painting require the same precautions; all these arts are of the same taste and tendency: as to music, we know that the ancients thought nothing was more pernicious to a well regulated republic, than to admit an *effeminate melody*: it enervates men, unbending and sensualizing their minds: languishing and passionate tones please only, by subjecting the soul to the seducement of the senses, till it becomes intoxicated by them. It was on this account, that the magistrates of Sparta broke all the instruments, the harmony of which was too delicate; and this was one of the most important parts of their policy. On the same account Plato strictly forbids all the luxurious tones of the Asiatic music; and christians, who ought never to pursue pleasure only for the sake of pleasure, are under much stronger obligations

[15] Fenelon is certainly fastidious when he censures the acquirement of the Italian language, which is one of the most soft and pleasing of any in modern Europe. Nor does it at all follow that a knowledge of the Italian language should lead to a knowledge of improper books—the same argument may be applied to any other language. *T.*

to guard themselves against these dangerous entertainments.

Poetry and music, *directed to their true end*, may be of excellent use to excite in the soul, lively and sublime sentiments of virtue. How many of the books of scripture of the poetical kind, according to all appearance were sung by the Hebrews. Songs were the first memorials which preserved more distinctly, the tradition of divine truths among men, before the invention of writing. We see how powerful music has been among the heathen nations, in elevating their minds above the sentiments of the vulgar: and the church has employed it,[16] for the consolation of her children, in celebrating the praises of God. We ought not therefore to abandon these arts, which the spirit of God himself hath consecrated.

Music and poetry employed on sacred subjects, would have a powerful influence in destroying the relish for profane pleasures. But while our present prejudices prevail, these arts cannot be cultivated without danger. Lose no time, therefore, in making a young woman who is strongly susceptible of these impressions, sensible of what charms may be found in music, even while it is confined to subjects of religion: if she has a good voice and a taste for music, never hope to keep her in ignorance of it; to forbid it will only increase her passion for it. It will be much better to give it a proper direction, than to endeavour to stifle it.

PAINTING is more easily convertible to good purposes; besides, it belongs in some degree to women; their needlework cannot properly be executed without it. I know they might be confined to employments that are simple and require no skill; but as I think we should contrive to employ the head and hands of women of condition at the same time, I could wish they had employments in which art and ingenuity might season their labours with some entertainment. Their work cannot have any real beauty, unless it be conducted by a knowledge of the rules of drawing; for want of which, what one sees in stuffs, lace, and embroidery, is done in an ill taste; all is confused; without design, without proportion.[17] These things are reckoned fine, because they cost a great deal of labour to those who work them, and a great deal of money to those who buy them. The lustre dazzles those who do

[16] An admirable sermon, "on the antiquity, use, and excellence, of church music," by Bishop Horne, may be seen among the 16 sermons separately published by that amiable prelate, in 8vo. Oxford, 1795, 2d edit. *T.*

[17] I do not think this applicable to the present system of fashion: women, in general display great taste in patterns, and great elegance in the adjustment of dress. *T.*

not closely examine, or are not skilful in these matters. The women on this subject have made rules of their own, which if any man should contest, he would be thought capricious and absurd. However, they might correct themselves by an attention to painting, and so be able, at a moderate expense, and to their great entertainment, to execute works of a noble variety and beauty, which would bid defiance to the caprice and uncertainty of fashion.

There is nothing which women ought to guard more against, or despise, than *living in idleness*. Let them consider that the first christians of whatever condition of life, all applied themselves to some employment, not as an amusement, but as a serious, useful, constant business. The order of nature, the penance imposed on the first man, and in him upon all his posterity, the great example which our Saviour Jesus Christ, hath set before us in this respect, all concur to engage us, each in his station, to a life of labour.

In the education of a young woman, her condition ought to be regarded, and the situation and cast of life she will probably move in. Take care that her expectations do not exceed her fortune and rank; if they do, they will cost her many sorrows; what would have made her happy, will become disgusting to her, if she has cast a wishful eye on a superior condition. If a girl is to live in the country, turn her attention betimes to the occupations of the country; keep her a stranger to the amusements of the town: shew her the blessings of a simple active life. If her situation be among the middle ranks of the town, let her not come near the people of the court; this intercourse will only serve to give her unbecoming and ridiculous airs: confine her within the bounds of her own station, and point out to her good examples among those of the same rank: form her mind to what will be the business of her life: teach her the management of a tradesman's family: the care that ought to be taken of his income, whether from returns out of the country, or rents of houses in the town: what belongs to the education of her children; in short the whole detail of business or of commerce, into which you foresee she may probably be thrown, when she is married.[18]

[18] What follows, in Fenelon, relating to the religious establishments of women, and taking the veil, is not here inserted—as being wholly inapplicable to the laws and customs of England.

Chapter XIII.

Of Governesses.

I foresee that this plan of education, will pass with many for a chimerical project: it requires, they will say, an uncommon share of discernment, patience, and skill, to carry it into execution: where are the governesses capable of following, or even understanding it? But it should be considered that when we are laying down rules for the best education that can be given to children, we are not to give imperfect rules; it is not matter of reprehension then, that in such an enquiry, we aim at what is most perfect. It is true, we cannot go so far in practice as our thoughts go upon paper, where they meet with no obstruction; but after all, though we are absolutely unable to arrive at perfection in this business, it will be far from useless to know what perfection is, and to attempt it at any rate; which is the best means of approaching it as nearly as we can. Besides, my rules do not proceed upon the supposition of any thing extraordinary in the disposition of children, or a concurrence of circumstances happily calculated for a perfect education; on the contrary I endeavour to apply remedies, to tempers naturally bad, or which have been spoilt: I calculate the common mistakes in education, and have recourse to the most simple methods of correcting, in the whole or in part, what has absolute need of correction.

It is true, you will not find in this little work, the means of giving success to an education neglected or ill conducted; but is there any thing strange in this? Is it not the most that one can wish, to obtain simple rules, by the observance of which, a good education may be acquired. I confess we may dispense, and do dispense generally, with much less than I propose; but it is likewise very obvious that children suffer materially by this neglect. The road I am pointing out, though tedious in appearance, is in reality the shortest, as it leads directly to the object we are in pursuit of. The other, which is that of *fear* and of a *superficial culture of the understanding*, short as it may seem, is in reality long; as it hardly ever attains to the *only true end of education*, which is to form the mind, and inspire it with a sincere love of virtue. The greater part of those who have gone this latter road, have to commence their journey anew, at a moment when their education seems finished; and after having passed the first years of their entrance into the world, in committing errors which are often irreparable, they are forced to learn from experience, and their own reflections, those maxims, of which that wretched and superficial education had left them in ignorance. It should be observed moreover, that the first services demanded in behalf of children, and which inexperienced people regard as oppressive and impracticable, will preserve them from troubles much more grievous; and remove obstacles which become insurmountable, in the course of an education less accurate and skilful.

Lastly it should be noticed that in order to execute this plan of education, the business does not consist so much in doing any thing which requires great talents, as in avoiding the gross errors previously enumerated. There will be often nothing more wanting than to be calm and patient with children: to be watchful over them: to inspire them with confidence: to give plain and intelligible answers to their little questions: to let their natural dispositions work in order to know them the better: and to correct them with temper, when they are mistaken, or in fault. It is not reasonable to expect that a good education can be conducted by a bad governess; it is enough to deliver rules which will give success to one, moderately qualified: of such a person it is not expecting too much that she be possessed of good sense, a mild temper, and the fear of God; such a one will find nothing in this treatise subtile or abstracted, and if she should not understand the whole of it, she will comprehend the substance at least; and that will be sufficient. Make her read it over many times, and be at the trouble of reading it with her; allow her the liberty of stopping you at any thing she does not understand, or of the truth of which she is not convinced; then let her put these instructions into practice, and if you should observe, that in talking to the child, she loses sight of the rules which she had agreed to follow, correct her privately in as mild a manner as possible. This application will be wearisome to you at first, but if you are the father or mother of the child, it is your *indispensable* duty. Besides, your difficulties will not be of long continuance: your governess, if she be sensible and well-disposed, will learn more of your method in a month by practice, than by long arguments; and she will soon be able to go on in the right way by herself. There will be this further circumstance to relieve you, that she will find in this little work, the principal topics of conversation, with children, upon the most important subjects already detailed for her; so that she will hardly have any thing to do but to follow them; thus she will possess a collection of the discourses she should hold with children, upon subjects the most difficult for them to understand; it is a kind of practical education which will be an easy guide to her.

You may likewise make excellent use of the *historical catechism* before-mentioned. Let the person you are forming to educate your children read it over so often, that it may be familiar to herself, and that she may enter into the spirit of this method of teaching. It must be acknowledged, however, that persons of even moderate talents for such services, are rarely to be met with; and yet nothing is to be done in education, without a proper instrument for the business; the commonest things cannot be done of themselves, and they are always ill done by improper people.—Choose therefore either out of your own family, or among your tenants, or friends, or from some well-ordered society, some young woman you think capable of being taught: apply yourself early to the forming of her for this employment: have her near you for some time, to make trial of her before you commit to her so important a trust. Five or six governesses trained in this manner, would soon be able to instruct a great number of others; many of these would probably fail, but out of a great number, we might always repair the loss, and not be so wretchedly compelled, as we continually are, to be seeking for a variety of teachers.

But though the difficulty of finding governesses is great; it must be confessed there is another yet greater, which is the *irregularity of parents*. All the rest will signify nothing, if *they* do not co-operate in the business: the foundation of every thing is giving their children *right notions* and *edifying examples*: and yet this is only to be found in very few families; in most, one sees nothing but confusion, perpetual changes, a heap of servants, who are not only quarreling with one another, but are the cause of disagreement among their masters and mistresses. What a woeful school is this for young children! The mother who passes her time in gaming, at plays, and in indiscreet conversations, very gravely complains that she cannot find a governess capable of bringing up her children; but what good can the best of educations confer on children, with the example of such a mother before them? One frequently sees parents who themselves carry their children to public diversions, and other amusements,[19] which cannot fail of giving them a disrelish for that serious and orderly course of life, in which these very parents wish to engage them: thus they mix poison with wholesome diet: they talk indeed of nothing but discretion, but at the same time they are agitating the flighty imagination of their children, by the violent impressions of music, and of passionate theatrical representations, which indispose them for application, give them a taste for what is passionate, and thereby make them think *innocent* pleasure *insipid*; and after all this still expect that the business of education shall go on well, and consider it as an irksome and austere thing, if it will not admit of *this mixture of good or evil*. Thus are they fond of the reputation of being anxious for the good education of their children, and yet are unwilling to be at the pains of complying with the most indispensable rules of it.

Let us conclude with the picture which the wise man has drawn of a *virtuous woman*.

> "Who can find a virtuous woman? for her price is far above rubies. The heart of her husband doth safely trust in her, so that he shall have no need of spoil. She will do him good and not evil all the days of her life. She seeketh wool, and flax, and worketh willingly with her hands. She is like the merchant ships, she bringeth her food from afar. She riseth also while it is yet night, and giveth meat to her household, and a proportion to her maidens. She considereth a field, and buyeth it; with the fruit of her hands she planteth a vineyard. She girdeth her loins with strength, and strengtheneth her arms. She perceiveth that her merchandize is good: her candle goeth not out by night. She layeth her hands to the spindle, and her hands hold the distaff. She stretcheth out her hand to the poor; yea, she reacheth forth her hands to the needy. She is not afraid of the snow for her household: for all her household are clothed with scarlet. She maketh herself coverings of tapestry, her clothing is silk and purple. Her

[19] I recommend the sensible mother, who has really the happiness of her daughter at heart, to peruse and reperuse the excellent observations on this head, which are to be found in a little pamphlet, lately published by the Rev. Mr. Owen; entitled "The Fashionable World Displayed."

> husband is known in the gates, when he sitteth among the elders of the land. She maketh fine linen, and selleth it, and delivereth girdles unto the merchant. Strength and honour are her clothing, and she shall rejoice in time to come. She openeth her mouth with wisdom, and in her tongue is the law of kindness. She looketh well to the ways of her household, and eateth not the bread of idleness. Her children arise up, and call her blessed; her husband also, and he praiseth her.
>
> Many daughters have done virtuously, but thou excellest them all. Favour is deceitful, and beauty is vain: but a woman that feareth the LORD, she shall be praised. Give her of the fruit of her hands, and let her own works praise her in the gates."

Though the great difference in manners, and the brevity and boldness of the figures, make this language obscure at first, yet the stile is so rich and animated, that we are soon charmed with it on examination. But what should be further remarked in it, is, that it is the authority of Solomon, the wisest of men; it is the Holy Spirit itself speaking in this lofty manner, to recommend to us, in the character of a woman of rank and fortune, SIMPLICITY OF MANNERS, DOMESTIC ECONOMY and INDUSTRY.

Printed by Libri Plureos GmbH in Hamburg,
Germany